SYDNEY

|CONDENSED|

nikki hall   dani valent

LONELY PLANET PUBLICATIONS
Melbourne • Oakland • London • Paris

contents

Lonely Planet Condensed – Sydney
Revised 1st edition – April 2000

Published by
Lonely Planet Publications Pty Ltd
A.C.N. 005 607 983
192 Burwood Rd, Hawthorn,
Victoria 3122, Australia

Lonely Planet Offices
Australia PO Box 617, Hawthorn, VIC 3122
USA 150 Linden St, Oakland, CA 94607
UK 10a Spring Place, London NW5 3BH
France 1 rue du Dahomey, 75011 Paris

Photographs
Many of the images in this guide are
available for licensing from Lonely Planet
Images. email: lpi@lonelyplanet.com.au

Thanks also to the Sydney Festival,
the National Library of Australia, Hotel Inter-
Continental and Tony Pyrzakowski.

Front cover photographs
Top: Opera House and Sydney Harbour
    Bridge (Christopher Groenhout)
Bottom: detail of Opera House
    (Simon Bracken)

ISBN 1 86450 045 X

text & maps © Lonely Planet 2000
photos © photographers as indicated 2000

Printed by The Bookmaker Pty Ltd
Printed in China

how to use this book

KEY TO SYMBOLS

✉	address	◷	opening hours
☎	telephone number	$	cost, entry charge
@	email/web site address	♿	wheelchair access
🚇	nearest train station	⚲	child-friendly
🚌	nearest bus route	✕	on-site or nearby eatery
⛴	nearest ferry wharf	🛏	local place to stay
🚗	car access	V	vegetarian, or with a good
ⓘ	tourist information		vegetarian selection

COLOUR-CODING

Each chapter has a different colour code which is reflected on the maps for quick reference.

MAPS & GRID REFERENCES

The fold-out maps on the front and back covers are numbered from 1 to 4. All sights and venues in the text have map references which indicate where to find them, eg (3, H4) means Map 3 , grid reference H4. When a map reference appears immediately after a name, the sight is labelled on the map; when it appears after an address (eg with most restaurants, hotels etc), only the street is marked.

PRICES

Multiple prices (eg $14/10/35) indicate adult/concession/family or group entry charges. Concession prices include child, pensioner and/or student discounts. Most family tickets cover 2 adults and 2 children.

WARNING & REQUEST

Things change – prices go up, schedules change, good places go bad and bad places improve or go bankrupt. So, if you find things better or worse, recently opened or long since closed, please tell us and help make the next edition even more accurate and useful. Everyone who writes to us will find their name and possibly excerpts from their correspondence in one of our publications (let us know if you *don't* want your letter published or your name acknowledged). They will also receive the latest issue of *Planet Talk*, our quarterly printed newsletter, or *Comet*, our monthly email newsletter. Subscriptions to both newsletters are free. The very best contributions will be rewarded with a free guidebook.

Send all correspondence to the Lonely Planet office closest to you (see p. 123).

Lonely Planet books provide independent advice. Lonely Planet does not accept advertising in guidebooks, nor payment in exchange for listing or endorsing any place or business. Lonely Planet writers do not accept discounts or payments in exchange for positive coverage of any sort.

facts about sydney

Sydney is stunning – a sure-fire finalist in a line-up of the world's most beautiful cities. Australia's capital in everything but name, and its oldest settlement, Sydney is blessed with sun-drenched natural attractions, dizzy skyscrapers, delicious and daring restaurants, super shopping and friendly folk. It's Australia's most vibrant, alluring and cosmopolitan city.

This is an outdoor city – think sparkling waterways, sandstone cliffs and hilly tree-lined streets. Everybody seems to be moving the body: they're yachting on the harbour, bushwalking through a national park, body-surfing at Bondi, sipping a heart-starter in a Darlinghurst cafe, strolling round The Rocks or parading – too buff for words – in the Mardi Gras.

Sydney's also been called the world's first postmodern city – a multicultural, hooked-in city of glossy surfaces – pluralist, chaotic, seductive and cynical. Most of Australia's immigrants touch down here, drawn by Sydney's pragmatic egalitarianism and gutsy opportunism. It is ironic that a settlement which began life as a British gulag has transformed in just over 200 years into one of the world's most tolerant and diverse societies.

Sydney has come a long way from its convict beginnings, but it still has a rough and ready energy which makes it an exciting place to visit. It offers an invigorating blend of the old and the new, the raw and the refined. Fight for the window seat on the flight in – you'll be landing somewhere special.

The Concourse Cafe is the place to watch the water traffic at Circular Quay.

HISTORY

Australia was the last great landmass to be 'discovered' by Europeans. However, the continent had already been inhabited for tens of thousands of years before the First Fleet arrived.

Bennelong

The volatile, troubled, puzzled relations between Bennelong, an Eora Aborigine, and the English are emblematic of much early contact.

Bennelong was kidnapped by Governor Phillip in 1789 in the hope that he would act as an interpreter and go-between. Though Bennelong took an initial liking to life at Government House, the following years were a parade of escape, recapture, anger, amity and misunderstanding.

Bennelong accompanied Phillip to England, where he met King George III and suffered to spend a couple of years. Upon returning to Australia, apparently embittered, Bennelong retreated from white contact.

Bennelong Point, where a house was built for his use and where the Opera House now stands, is named after him.

*James Nagle's 1798 engraving **Ben-nil-long**, depicting Bennelong in his full western finery. By permission of the National Library of Australia, NK 9503.*

Aboriginal Society

The Sydney area was the ancestral home of the Eora tribe, whose territory extended from Botany Bay to Pittwater. There are some 2000 Aboriginal rock engraving sites in the Sydney area, and many of Sydney's suburbs have Aboriginal names.

When the British arrived at Sydney Cove, over 200 years ago, there were about 3000 Aborigines living in the environs of what is now Sydney, and approximately 300,000 in Australia. Under the colonial system Aborigines were stripped of any legal rights to the land they once lived on, many were driven away by force, and thousands succumbed to diseases brought by white people.

European Settlement

Europeans first reached Australia in the 16th century: Portuguese navigators were followed by Dutch explorers and the enterprising English pirate William Dampier. Captain James Cook sailed the entire length of the eastern coast in 1770, claiming the continent for the British and naming it New South Wales. On their return home, Joseph Banks (a naturalist on Cook's voyage) suggested that Britain could solve overcrowding problems in its prisons by transporting convicts to the other side of the world.

The British Government embraced the idea, and in 1787 the First Fleet set sail from Portsmouth, England, under the command of Captain Arthur Phillip, who was to become the colony's first governor. The fleet comprised 11 ships, 759 convicts, 4 companies of marines and supplies for 2 years. Phillip arrived in Botany Bay on 26 January 1788, but soon moved north to Sydney Cove, where there was better land and water.

Colonial Expansion

In 1800, there were still only 2 small settlements in the Australian colony – Sydney Cove and Norfolk Island in the Pacific Ocean. The vast interior of the continent was explored in the ensuing 40 years.

Free settlers were increasingly attracted to New South Wales as more areas were opened up and the transportation of convicts ended (1840). But it was the discovery of gold in the 1850s that irrevocably changed the face of the colony. The huge influx of migrants and the injection of wealth boosted the economy and altered colonial social structures.

The 20th Century

During the 1890s, calls for the separate colonies to federate became increasingly strident, and on 1 January 1901 NSW became a state of the new Australian nation. However, Australia's legal ties and its loyalty to Britain remained strong.

WWII marked the beginning of Australia's shift of allegiance from Britain towards the USA, after the US defeated the Japanese in the Battle of the Coral Sea and thus saved Australia from possible invasion.

Postwar immigrants, mainly from the UK, Ireland and the Mediterranean, brought new growth and prosperity to Australia during the 1950s and 60s, and Sydney's urban development rapidly spread into the western hinterland.

The face of Sydney changed again during the Vietnam War, as American GIs flooded the city for R&R. Kings Cross excelled in providing sleazy entertainment for the US troops, while Sydneysiders soaked up all things American – from hamburgers and Coca-Cola to the burgeoning hippie and peace movements.

The booming economy of the 1980s saw Sydney flush with new skyscrapers, and the 1988 bicentenary celebrations were a controversial marker of the British landing.

Ice-capades

Until the 1860s, ice was shipped to Australia from as far away as the eastern USA, where it was cut from lakes and packed in sawdust. When the chilly load reached Sydney it was stored at Ice House in Ice St, Darlinghurst. In 1862, the unthinkable happened – Ice House burnt down, the victim of lads with fireworks celebrating the Queen's birthday. Sydney's first commercial ice making plant was built the next year.

Sydney Today

Today Sydney cuts a confident path between the buzziness of commercial success and the breezier pleasures of life in a city where 'fun' isn't yet a four-letter word. As host to the 2000 Olympic Games, Sydney finds itself centre of the world stage at the beginning of the new millennium. Although the building boom brought on by Olympics preparations is viewed with a mix of Sydney bravado and typical Australian cynicism, everyone wants to be here. House prices are rocketing, a third airport runway has been built and more and more travellers are back for a second, or third, visit.

ORIENTATION

Sydney is centred on the harbour of Port Jackson but Greater Sydney sprawls over 1800 sq km, encompassing Botany Bay in the south (where the airport is), abutting the foothills of the Blue Mountains in the west and the fringes of the national parks near Broken Bay in the north. The city is hilly, and its layout complicated by the harbour's numerous bays and headlands.

The harbour divides Sydney into northern and southern halves, with the Sydney Harbour Bridge and the Harbour Tunnel joining the 2 shores. The city centre and most places of interest are south of the harbour.

East of the city centre are the inner-city suburbs of Darlinghurst (gym bodies), Kings Cross (sleazy) and Paddington (pink and pretty). Further east again, and stretching to South Head, are exclusive suburbs such as Double Bay (Range Rovers) and Vaucluse (Volvos). To the south-east of these are the ocean-beach suburbs of Bondi (short board) and Coogee (boogie board).

West of the centre is reinvigorated Pyrmont, and the peninsula suburbs of Glebe (bohemian) and Balmain (trendy). The inner west includes grungy Newtown and Leichhardt with its Italian bistros. The middle-class North Shore stretches from the Harbour Bridge to the edge of Pittwater.

Flushed with Pride

The Sydney Olympics site at Homebush Bay is partially solar powered and has been built on energy saving, conservationist principles. Volunteers – 10,000 of them – were summoned to Homebush during the preparations, and stationed at each of the site's 10,000 toilets. At a siren signal, they each flushed to see if the system could cope. Thankfully, it did.

ENVIRONMENT

When you start with such a glorious setting, you have a lot of incentive to keep things nice. Sydney's residents make as much mess as other city people, but they're a pretty environmentally sensitive bunch. Households and businesses increasingly recycle paper, glass and plastic. Parks and bushland in and around Sydney act as animal and plant habitats, recreation reserves and the city's 'lungs'.

Sydney's beaches are generally clean but can become polluted after heavy rainfall. Millions of dollars have been spent installing pollution traps and litter booms to prevent rubbish flowing along stormwater drains, but it's still best not to swim in the harbour beaches for 3 days after rain. In August 1998, Sydneysiders had to boil their drinking water when heavy rain swept animal excreta into the city's main reservoir; generally tap water is potable.

Sydney's love affair with the car and the city's high humidity mean that air pollution can be extreme. Those with allergies and asthma should check daily air pollution levels in newspaper weather sections. The world's biggest ozone hole – a gaping 26 million sq km – is above southern Australia: don't go out without sunblock.

GOVERNMENT & POLITICS

Sydney is the capital of NSW and the seat of the state government, which conducts its business at Parliament House in Macquarie St. The system of government is a combination of the British Westminster and US systems.

There are 2 main political groupings in NSW: the Australian Labor Party and a coalition of the Liberal and National parties. At the time of writing, the Labor Party holds government and Bob Carr is Premier. Minor parties with parliamentary representation include the Greens, the Christian Democratic Party and the Shooters Party. The last election, comfortably won by Labor, was held in March 1999.

Most Sydneysiders are wryly cynical about state politics – there's not a great deal of love around for Bob Carr's Labor machine, but the Liberal/National coalition was widely perceived as being too incompetent to risk in office. Recent major political issues have included the Olympics (scandals over ticket sales and dismay about overspending), drug law reform and rehab (particularly heroin and marijuana) and air traffic noise over the inner city.

ECONOMY

Sydney is Australia's chief commercial, financial and industrial centre. It is also an important transport centre, with 2 harbours – Sydney Harbour (also called Port Jackson) and, about 15km south, Botany Bay – plus Australia's busiest airport and a network of roads and rail. Most of Australia's foreign trade is conducted in Sydney and NSW, and oil refining is a major local industry.

About half the workforce is employed in manufacturing and the rest in services such as transport, finance, retail and tourism, the latter being a particularly thriving industry.

Richard I'Anson

Absolute Waterfront! There's nothing more desirable in Sydney than a view of blue.

SOCIETY & CULTURE

Sydney has a population of about 4 million out of the Australian total of 19 million. It's a multicultural city, although before WWII most Sydneysiders were predominantly of British and Irish descent. That changed dramatically in the aftermath of the war, with large migrations from Italy and Greece, as well as the former Yugoslavia, Lebanon and Turkey.

Hey True Blue

If you come to Sydney in search of a real, or 'true-blue', Australian you'll find the place crawling with them. He or she may be a Lebanese cafe owner, an English used-car salesperson, an Aboriginal magistrate, a Malaysian architect or a Greek greengrocer. And they'll be gay, straight, sporty or beer-gutted. You will find them in pubs, on beaches, at barbecues, at art galleries or mowing their suburban lawns. And though you may meet a Mick (Crocodile) Dundee or two telling tall stories, you probably won't come across anyone with a pet kangaroo.

Asian migration to Australia began in the 1850s when Chinese migrants were attracted by gold, but there were also large influxes of Vietnamese after the Vietnam War. More recently, immigrants have come from Thailand, Cambodia, the Philippines and Hong Kong. Today, Chinese is Sydney's second language.

Aboriginal Society

Although non-Aborigines are at last recognising the complexities of indigenous culture, many people are still intolerant of urban Aborigines, who maintain strong links with traditional ways. This causes frequent misunderstandings, and urban Aborigines are still often labelled as troublemakers because they don't conform to the norms of modern Australia. Sydney's inner-city suburb of Redfern has a large and vital Koori population (many Aborigines in south-eastern Australia describe themselves as Koories), though trendification is forcing many away from the area.

Etiquette

Sydney moves fast but tries to stay relaxed. The atmosphere is laid-back and the people generally friendly and helpful. Smokers should note that restaurants sometimes have 'no smoking' areas and some outdoor areas at sporting arenas are smoke-free. Mobile (cell) phone etiquette is forgiving – 4 people at a cafe talking *only* to one another isn't very Sydney; someone is bound to be chatting on the phone. However, be sure to turn your phone off during business meetings, in theatres and cinemas.

Doing business in Sydney tends to be pretty straightforward – candour is likely to get you further than smooth-talking obfuscation, though it never hurts to have insider connections. A lot of bonding, gossiping and character assessment occurs in the pub – if an associate invites you out for a 'cold one' (a beer), it's not just a wind down, it's often an essential part of the process. Business dress is formal with a definite allowance for individuality and the fact that you may have just been for a surf.

Arts

Painting Australian light and colour were not rendered in a naturalistic fashion until the late 1880s. Tom Roberts and fellow Melburnian Arthur Streeton established an artists' camp at Little Sirius Cove in Mosman in 1891 which became a focal point for Sydney artists.

In the 1940s, there was a flowering of predominantly expressionist art with painters such as Sidney Nolan, Arthur Boyd, Albert Tucker and Russell Drysdale.

Sydney artist Brett Whiteley, who died in 1992, was an internationally celebrated *enfant terrible* who painted luscious, colourful canvases, often with distorted Bacon-like figures. His paintings of Sydney Harbour and Lavender Bay are particularly powerful; his studio has been preserved as a gallery (p. 37) in Surry Hills.

Brett Whiteley Studio – insight into the weird and wonderful works of one of Australia's great artists.

Literature While Australian painters in the 1880s were developing their own style, a number of writers were creating fiction with a distinctive Australian flavour. Despite the early propensity for tales of masculine life in the bush, it was a woman, Miles Franklin (1879-1954), who wrote *My Brilliant Career* (1901), once described as 'the very first Australian novel'.

Modern Australian authors are now some of the most highly regarded in the world. Writers of international stature include Patrick White (Nobel Prize winner 1973); Thomas Keneally (Booker Prize winner 1982) and Peter Carey (Booker Prize winner 1988). Other notable authors include David Malouf, Frank Moorhouse, Rodney Hall, Tim Winton, Helen Garner, Elizabeth Jolley and Robert Drewe.

Dance The Australian Ballet, the national ballet company, is considered one of the finest in the world. It performs a mixed program of classical and modern pieces and usually presents 4 ballets a year at the Opera House.

Under the guidance of its artistic director, Graeme Murphy, the Sydney Dance Company (SDC) has become Australia's leading contemporary dance company. It also performs at the Opera House. The acclaimed Bangarra Dance Theatre regularly performs Aboriginal song and dance, fusing ancient and modern styles.

Music In Sydney you can hear everything from world class opera to grungy pub bands and live electronic acts. See pages 87-100 for a full run-down of entertainment options.

Local performers play at pubs and small clubs around the city, while touring big-name international acts can be seen at the Entertainment Centre in Darling Harbour, Selina's at Coogee Beach, the Metro in George St and the Hordern Pavilion at Moore Park.

Sydney has a flourishing dance music scene, with good local DJs and frequent international acts. There are clubs and dance parties catering to every sub-genre, from hip-hop to drum & bass, techno and house.

Conservatorium of Music

A healthy jazz scene centres on city venues such as the Basement, the Harbourside Brasserie and the Strawberry Hills Hotel. Classical music can be heard at the Opera House, the universities and several venues utilised by the Conservatorium of Music.

The Sydney Symphony Orchestra is Australia's largest orchestra. It performs over 140 concerts a year, many at the Opera House. Opera Australia, the national company, is based at the Opera House for 7 months of the year.

These diverse strands of Sydney's musical life are brought together each January in the Domain during the 3-week Sydney Festival (p. 92).

Film Australia's first cinema was opened in Sydney in 1896, a year after the Lumière brothers opened the world's first movie-house in Paris. Maurice Sestier, one of the Lumières' photographers, came to Australia and made the first films in the streets of Sydney and Melbourne.

Today, Sydney's film industry is thriving. Contemporary directors and producers who have spent significant time in the city include Baz Luhrmann *(Romeo & Juliet)*, Jane Campion *(The Piano)*, Gillian Armstrong, George Miller, Peter Weir *(Truman Show)*, Bruce Beresford and Rachel Perkins, a young Aboriginal filmmaker.

A recent boost to the scene is the opening of Rupert Murdoch's Fox Studios at Moore Park. *Shine, Babe, Babe II, Face/Off, The Matrix, The Thin Red Line, Truman Show* and *Mission Impossible II* have all used the postproduction facilities at Fox. See page 57 for tours of the site.

It's not all big bucks and an eye on the Oscars though. Tropfest (p. 97), a made-to-order short film contest, is one of Sydney's hottest celluloid events.

highlights

Most of Sydney's attractions scream to be included here – they're either so stunning as to be unmissable or they're purpose-built visitor magnets. Others have accrued top status more naturally – they're local hangouts with a special charm or flavour, rewarding to visit for the insight they give into how the city ticks. The following selection is a blend of the bleeding obvious and the slightly tucked away, many in the city centre or nearby inner suburbs.

Stopping Over?

One Day Walk around Sydney Cove to the Opera House and Royal Botanic Gardens. Visit the Museum of Contemporary Art and wander around The Rocks. Take a predinner stroll up the Harbour Bridge steps and head back to The Rocks for dinner.

Two Days Get out on the harbour: take a ferry to Taronga Zoo, or to Manly for a swim and a scenic walk. Dine out in Darlinghurst and go for a dance or nightcap in Paddington's nightclubs and bars.

Three Days Check out the fashions and shops in Oxford St, then head to the Queen Victoria Building on George St for more shopping. Ride to the top of nearby Sydney Tower for panoramic views and dine at the tower's revolving restaurant.

Richard I'Anson

Great Views

- the highest view in Sydney is from **Sydney Tower** (p. 26)
- the **Harbour Bridge** (p. 21) offers excellent views
- combine a fluffy duck with an eyefull at the ANA Hotel's **Horizons Cocktail Lounge** (p. 102)
- for a sea-level view of the Opera House and harbour, walk to **Mrs Macquarie's Point** (p. 20)
- for the best harbour views of all, catch a **ferry** (p. 56-7, 112)

Sydney Lowlights

Darling Harbour

While its excellent attractions and some fab Cockle Bay restaurants almost redeem it, this massive area feels overplanned, sterile and icky. It has been tinkered with and tacked onto since it opened in the late 1980s, but it's never been quite right.

The Rocks

Though this is one of the city's top attractions, it gets a boo-boo prize for its contrived Australiana stores – not every visitor wants to go home with a wombat keyring.

Simon Bracken

BONDI BEACH   (2, J14)

Although it's Australia's most famous beach, Bondi Beach isn't super glam. In pre-rollerblade days, Bondi's flavour came from its blend of Jews, Italians and beach loving Anglo-Aussies. As it's become more fashionable,

INFORMATION

- Bondi Junction, then bus 380, 382, 389 & L82
- ① the Festival of the Winds in September features kite flying contests and kite making workshops

the beach bunnies are wearing a lot more linen, you have to pay for parking, and trendy snack-bars (hankering after yabbie pizza?) line the main drag. Happily, the mix of old-timers, expats, working travellers, Japanese tourists and surfers is a harmonious one: all are bonded by their love of the water.

The main reason for coming is the beach, where you can swim, surf or just hang out. If the ocean's too rough for swimming there are salt-water swimming pools at either end, which are also suitable for young children. **Bondi Pavilion** has changing rooms and showers, and is also a theatre, gallery and concert venue.

If you walk a short way north of Bondi Beach, you can see **Aboriginal rock engravings** at the Royal Sydney Golf Course in North Bondi (in fact, the name 'bondi' comes from the Aboriginal word for the sound of the surf).

A beautiful coastal walking path leads south to the beaches at Tamarama, Bronte and Coogee and through the **Waverley Cemetery** (2, K13) where writer Henry Lawson and cricketer Victor Trumper are among the interred.

DON'T MISS
- clifftop coastal walking path
- people-watching at a Campbell Parade cafe

Watch out for the Iceberg! The hardy souls of Bondi's Iceberg Club dip daily regardless of the season.

CHINATOWN (3, N5)

Fuelled by an influx of money from Hong Kong, Sydney's Chinatown is booming. A dense concentration of restaurants and shops in and around **Dixon St**, it caters to the Chinese community and lovers of all things Asian.

Chinatown is particularly exciting during Chinese New Year (late January/early February) when the streets are crowded with sideshows, musicians and stalls selling everything from good-luck tokens to black sesame ice cream burgers. Seeing a jaunty dragon breathing paper fire is almost a certainty.

At any time of year you can spend a small fortune at an outstanding Chinese restaurant, or chow down for next to nothing in a food hall. Weekend yum cha is popular but be prepared to queue for a table at some of the more popular places. Thai, Vietnamese,

INFORMATION

🚉 Central, monorail, SLR
✕ see page 75

Chinese Immigration

The first Chinese came to Australia around 1840 when convict shipments stopped and labouring jobs were freely available. Many more came out during the gold rush; but after the anti-Asian 'White Australia Policy' was enacted in 1861, the Chinese population declined.

Sydney's Chinese community gravitated to Dixon St around 1870; it quickly became a busy commercial centre notorious for its opium dens and gambling.

Japanese and Korean eateries are also common, and if you head north to **Liverpool St**, there's even a cluster of Spanish tapas bars.

Shopping in Chinatown is fun too – whether you're after some incense or a killer deal on a mobile phone, you'll find it. Chinatown also encompasses **Paddy's Market** (p. 62) – a Sydney institution that offers the usual market fare at rock-bottom prices.

The Chinese Garden of Friendship (p. 16), just over the Liverpool St footbridge in Darling Harbour, is a peaceful spot to relax.

Lion statues guard the entrance to the Chinese Garden of Friendship.

DARLING HARBOUR (3, M3)

This huge, purpose-built waterfront leisure park on the city's western edge was once a thriving dockland with factories, warehouses and shipyards lining Cockle Bay.

These days, Darling Harbour is home to the excellent Sydney Aquarium (p. 36) and Powerhouse Museum (p. 35), both full of fascinating interactive displays, the Australian National Maritime Museum (p. 34), the touristy Harbourside shopping mall, an IMAX theatre (p. 96) with a giant eight-storey screen, Segaworld (p. 41) for the kids and the contrived but tasty Cockle Bay Wharf development.

The exquisite **Chinese Garden of Friendship** (☎ 9281 6863; open 9.30am-5.30pm) has been built according to the principles of yin and yang (balance) – think of it as a 10 hectare oasis of tranquility. The teahouse overlooking the lotus pond is a pleasant spot to stop for tea and Chinese cakes.

In the immediate vicinity is **Pyrmont** (3, L2), home to the Sydney Fish Market (p. 71) and the playground of bigger fish, the Star City Casino (p. 100). Darling Harbour and Pyrmont are serviced by monorail and SLR. A dinky people mover connects the sights ($2.50/1.50).

INFORMATION

- 🚊🚋 Darling Harbour
- 💲 Superticket $37.40/ 24.40 gives entry to several sights, plus a harbour cruise, monorail ride and a meal; valid for 1mth
- ⓘ Visitors Centre
- ☎ 9286 0111
- ♿ good
- ✗ Chinta Ria (p. 76), Wokpool (p. 77), Harbourside food court

Simon Bracken

DON'T MISS
- Sydney Aquarium • IMAX • Australian National Maritime Museum
- Chinese Garden of Friendship • Powerhouse Museum

Simon Bracken

Sydney Convention Centre, the Novotel and the Ibis Hotel line the waterfront at Darling Harbour.

KINGS CROSS & SURROUNDS   (4)

'The Cross' is a bizarre cocktail of strip joints, drugs and backpacker hostels, with a handful of classy restaurants, designer cafes and gorgeous guesthouses thrown in. It attracts an odd mix of low-life, sailors, travellers and suburbanites looking for a big night out.

Sometimes the razzle-dazzle has a sideshow appeal; sometimes walking up Darlinghurst Rd is as appetising as finding a cockroach in your cornflakes.

Away from the spruikers and the spew, though, everything becomes a little bit delightful and the contiguous neighbourhoods of **Elizabeth Bay** and **Potts Point**, to the north, are just lovely.

Kings Cross was a place of grand homes from the 1810s, but when money dried up in the 1840s the larger holdings were subdivided and the terraces which are now the architectural mainstay of the area were built. In the 1930s, a raffish element moved in, hats and elbows cocked, and during the Vietnam War era, the Cross became the vice centre of Australia.

Remnants of Victorian, Edwardian and Deco architecture are apparent in lovely tree-lined streets such as **Victoria St** (4, C4) and along Llankelly Place, Springfield Ave and Roslyn St (4, C5). Many of these buildings owe their continued existence to local protests against developers (called 'Green Bans') in the 1970s. The area's most beautiful building is **Elizabeth Bay House** (p. 34).

INFORMATION

🚆 Kings Cross
🚌 311, 330, 323-7, 365. 366, 387, L24
ⓘ Currency Exchange kiosk (4, C5) in Springfield Ave provides tourist information and books tours
℮ www.ssyd.nsw.gov.au; www.kingscross.nsw. gov.au

Contrasts of the Cross: sex for sale (top) and the genteel Elizabeth Bay House (above).

Woolloomooloo, wedged between the city and the Cross, is affectionately known as the 'loo'. At the bottom of the McElhone Stairs, on Cowper Wharf Rd, you'll find one of Sydney's more eccentric comestible institutions, **Harry's Cafe de Wheels** (p. 85). No visit to Sydney is complete without tasting one of Harry's pies 'n' mushy peas. Next door is **Finger Wharf**, a new boardwalk with harbourside cafes, bars and restaurants.

DON'T MISS
• Elizabeth Bay House • a pie from Harry's Cafe de Wheels
• beautiful tree-lined Victoria St

MANLY (2, C14)

One of the highlights of a visit to Sydney is taking the ferry to Manly – it's the single best way to get on the harbour and drink in those famous views. Traversing the length of the harbour east of the Harbour Bridge, it's a half-hour trip by ferry and 15 minutes by JetCat.

INFORMATION

- from Circular Quay
- ⓘ Visitor Information Centre, North Steyne (☎ 9977 1088); weekend craft market in Sydney Rd; Manly International Jazz Festival in October
- ℮ vic@manly.nsw.gov.au; www.manly.nsw.gov. au; www.pcn.com.au

Once you're there, Manly has all the trappings of a brash holiday resort. Perched on the narrow peninsula ending at the dramatic cliffs of North Head, it boasts both ocean and harbour beaches linked by the birdshit-spattered Corso. Though **the Corso** has more $2 shops and bad cappuccinos than is probably decent, it does attract some talented buskers and has ice cream worth a lick.

On the harbour side is **Oceanworld** (p. 36), a wonderful walk-in aquarium, and the **Manly Art Gallery & Museum** which concentrates on beachy local history.

You can gulp down fantastic views of the ocean, harbour and city sky-line at **North Head** (2, D15), the Sydney Harbour entrance about 3km south of Manly. The **Quarantine Station** nearby housed suspected and real disease carriers from 1832 to 1984 and many people died there. The station is reputedly haunted and there are ghost tours 4 times a week, including special ghost tours for kids (p. 41). Non-ghostly tours run 5 times a week; call ☎ 9977 6522 for bookings.

The **Scenic Walkway** (p. 51) west of Manly towards The Spit Bridge is one of Sydney's loveliest.

DON'T MISS
- the 10km Manly Scenic Walkway • a spooky ghost tour at the Quarantine Station

Lifeguards patrol Manly's beaches – it's best to swim between the red and yellow flags to remain under their watchful gaze.

PADDINGTON & SURROUNDS (4)

Paddington, or 'Paddo', 4km east of the city centre, is a fine example of unplanned urban restoration. Its fascinating jumble of beautifully restored terraces tumble down steeply sloping streets, and the suburb is full of just-so shops and restaurants, art galleries, bookshops and interesting people.

Looking at Paddington today, it's hard to believe that in 1860 it was rugged bushland. By 1895, it was covered in terrace houses and by WWII it was the worst slum in Australia. European migrants began prettying it up postwar; in the 1960s it became fashionable and by the 1990s it was out of reach of all but the lucky and the loaded.

INFORMATION

🚌 378, 380, 382, L82
ⓘ a 'Guide & Map to Art Galleries in Paddington & Inner City' is available at shops and galleries in the area

You can wander through Paddington's streets and winding laneways any time, although it's best from around 10am Saturday, when **Paddington Bazaar** (p. 62), in the grounds of the Uniting Church at the corner of Newcombe and Oxford Sts (4, J7), is in full swing. The crowds are as interesting as the myriad stalls.

The lifeblood of Paddington and nearby Darlinghurst is **Oxford St**, one of the more exciting places for late-night action. It's a strip of shops, cafes, bars and nightclubs, whose flamboyance and spirit are largely attributed to the vibrant and vocal gay community. The route of the Sydney Gay & Lesbian Mardi Gras parade passes this way. **Taylor Square** (4, F2), at the junction of Oxford, Flinders and Bourke Sts, is the area's social hub.

Darlinghurst is a vital area of trendy, self-conscious cool leavened by the old-school hip in Stanley St's Little Italy (4, D2) and the buckets of dhal slopped out by Indian fast food restaurants. Darlinghurst is also home to the Sydney Jewish Museum (p. 36).

Centennial Park is at the eastern end of Oxford St (4, K9). It is large and leafy and dotted with people walking, playing sport, cycling, rollerblading, horseriding or simply sitting under a tree with a book or a sweetheart.

For a walking tour of Paddington, see page 49.

Gentrified terraces in Hargrave Street, Paddington

ROYAL BOTANIC GARDENS (3, H9)

The Royal Botanic Gardens were established in 1816, and include the site of the colony's first vegetable patch. Today it has a magnificent collection of South Pacific plant life, an old-fashioned rose garden, an arid garden featuring cacti and succulents, and a dark, dank bat colony.

INFORMATION

- 🚈🚌🚢 Circular Quay
- 🕐 8am-sunset
- 💲 free
- ℹ️ Visitors Centre (☎ 9231 8125; 9.30am-4.30pm); free guided walks from 10.30am daily; audio tours available ($7; 90 mins); occasional guided bush tucker and Aboriginal legends walks
- 📧 www.rbgsyd.gov.au
- ♿ good; Visitors Centre maps show access
- ✕ Botanic Gardens Restaurant & Cafe, Pavilion on the Park, Palace Gate Kiosk

There's a tropical Australian collection housed in a funky **glass pyramid**; it includes monsoonal, woodland and rainforest plants. Another steamy greenhouse has rampant climbers and trailers from a number of the world's rainforests.

Mrs Macquarie's Point has been a lookout since at least 1810, when Elizabeth Macquarie, wife of Governor Lachlan Macquarie, had a stone chair hewn into the rock so she could watch ships entering the harbour and keep an eye on hubby's construction projects just across Farm Cove.

Government House (3, E8), in the north-western part of the gardens, is a romantic Gothic building and one of the only grand old homes which has hung onto its lovely English-style grounds and uninterrupted harbour views. The sometimes impressive, sometimes fussy furniture reflects the tastes of a procession of governors and their wives. It's open Fri-Sun 10am-3pm; admission is free.

The **Domain**, a large, grassy area linking the Botanic Gardens to Hyde Park, was set aside by Governor Phillip in 1788 for public recreation. It also contained Australia's first farm. On Sunday afternoons it's the gathering place for impassioned soapbox speakers who do their best to entertain or enrage their listeners. It's also the setting for **Carols by Candlelight** at

Sydney's answer to IM Pei's Louvre creation

Christmas and free summer concerts (p. 94).

In summer, theatre and cinema performances are held in the gardens. For children, special shows and educational theatre workshops are organised periodically at the Kid's Branch (p. 41). A trackless train does a circuit of the gardens if you've outdone yourself with strolling.

SYDNEY HARBOUR BRIDGE   (3, B7)

From the northern end of The Rocks, the imposing 'old coat hanger' crosses the harbour at one of its narrowest points, linking the southern and northern shores and joining central Sydney with the satellite business district of North Sydney. The bridge has always been a popular icon – partly because of its sheer size and symmetry, partly because of its function in uniting the city, and partly because it kept a lot of people in work during the Depression in the 1920s.

The 2 halves of the mighty arch were built out from each shore, supported by cranes. In 1932, after 9 years of work, when the ends of the arches were only centimetres apart and ready to be bolted together, a gale blew and winds of more than 100km/h set them swaying. Thankfully the bridge survived and the arch was soon completed.

The bridge cost $20 million, a bargain by modern standards, but it took until 1988 to pay it off.

Staircases lead up to the bridge from both ends and a footpath runs right across. If the view from the footpath isn't enough, you can climb 200 stairs inside the south-east pylon or join the ant-line of bridge climbers for panoramic views of the harbour. A **museum** (☎ 9247 3408) in the south-east pylon is open 10am-5pm daily.

INFORMATION

- ✉ access from The Rocks (Cumberland St) and the North Shore (near Milsons Point train station)
- 🚆 Circular Quay, Milsons Point
- ⑤ free for pedestrians, $2 toll for city-bound vehicles
- ⓘ you can organise to climb the bridge (see p. 40)
- ♿ no

did you know?

- 1400 workers took 9 years to build the bridge
- 16 builders died in construction accidents
- it takes 10 years and 30,000 litres of paint to coat it
- it weighs nearly 53,000 tonnes
- 6 million rivets hold it together
- one of those rivets is said to be solid gold
- cockroaches and rats scurry across the bridge at night

The vital link between north and south, the Sydney Harbour Bridge carries thousands of train and car commuters daily, plus a few pedestrians.

SYDNEY HARBOUR (2)

The harbour is the focal point of the city, and its beaches, coves, bays and waterside parks offer welcome relief from the rigours of urban life. Criss-crossed by ferries and carpeted by yachts on weekends, it is both the city's

Richard I'Anson

playground and a major port. The harbour's multiple sandstone headlands, dramatic cliffs, rocky islands and stunning bays and beaches stretch some 20km inland to join the mouth of the Parramatta River. The most scenic area is on the ocean side of the bridge.

The **Sydney Harbour National Park** protects the scattered pockets of bushland around the harbour and offers good walking tracks. The best way to experience the harbour is to go sailing, but if you're lacking nautical skills there are plenty of other ways to enjoy it. Try catching the ferry to Manly (p. 18), swimming at Nielsen Park (2, F13), walking from Manly to The Spit Bridge (p. 51), dining with a view at Watsons Bay (p. 84), Rose Bay (2, G13), Balmoral (2, D12) or Circular Quay, or cruising to the heads aboard the *Bounty* (p. 57).

Five islands in Sydney Harbour are also part of the national park. **Clark Island** (2, G11), off Darling Point, **Shark Island** (2, F12), off Rose Bay, and **Rodd Island** (2, G6), in Iron Cove, make great picnic getaways. **Goat Island** (2, F9), once a notorious convict working site, is now used as a setting for *Water Rats*, one of Australia's most popular TV serials.

Fort Denison (2, F11) is a small fortified island off Mrs Macquarie's

Christopher Groenhout

Point. Originally used as a punishment 'cell' to isolate troublesome convicts (when it earned the nickname 'Pinchgut' because of the meagre rations), it was fortified in the mid-19th century during the Crimean War amid fears of a Russian invasion. The NPWS at Cadman's Cottage runs tours to Goat Island (p. 40) and Fort Denison ($12/8); to visit the others you must book through the NPWS ($3 per person) and then organise your own transport, such as a water taxi.

The defining human contributions to the harbour

The southern arm of the entrance to Sydney Harbour is home to **Watsons Bay** (2, E14), a popular beach nestled on the harbour side of the peninsula. The suburb has a pleasant village atmosphere, with antique shops and cottages, and it's surrounded by part of Sydney Harbour National Park. On the Pacific Ocean side of the peninsula is **the Gap**, with its dramatic cliff-top lookout – a popular spot for catching sunrises and sunsets (it's also a notorious suicide spot).

On the harbour north of Watsons Bay are 2 small but fashionable beaches – **Lady Bay** (p. 43) is a mainly gay, nudist beach, while **Camp Cove** (p. 43), the spot where Arthur Phillip first landed, is popular with families and topless bathers. At the tip of the peninsula is **South Head** (2, E14), with great views across the harbour to North Head and Middle Head. The boat trip back to the city is wonderful.

There's a fine short walk round South Head, beginning at Camp Cove and passing Lady Bay, Inner South Head and the Gap, ending at Outer South Head.

After you've stretched your legs and had a bite to eat, catch the ferry (afternoons only) or a water taxi back to town.

A humble member of Sydney's flotilla at Watsons Bay

DON'T MISS
- fish & chips at Doyles, Watsons Bay
- sunrise or sunset at the Gap • a harbour island picnic or tour

Sydney beachgoers are spoilt for choice. If the rough and tumble of the coastal beaches doesn't suit, try one of the harbour beaches such as Camp Cove (above).

SYDNEY OPERA HOUSE (3, D8)

Australia's most recognisable icon sits dramatically on **Bennelong Point** on the eastern headland of Circular Quay. It's a truly memorable place to see a performance, listen to a free outdoor concert or sit under a cafe umbrella and watch harbour life go by. The Opera House itself looks good from any angle, but the view from a ferry coming into Circular Quay is one of the best.

Construction started in 1959, and the Opera House was officially opened in 1973, after a tumultuous series of personality clashes, technical difficulties and delays. Dane Jørn Utzon's design is said to have been inspired by everything from palm fronds, orange segments, shells and sails to Mayan temples, and has been compared to the rare sight of white turtles engaging in sexual congress.

The Opera House has 4 auditoriums where dance, theatre, concerts and opera are staged (see p. 94 for details). Many events sell out quickly, but there are often restricted view or standing room tickets available for $25-30 from 9am on the day of performance. One Sunday a month, there's **free entertainment** outside on the 'prow'. There's a regular Sunday **art and craft market** (p. 62) on the Concourse.

The bi-monthly *Opera House Diary* is available free at the Opera House. For kids, there are concerts during school holidays as part of the Bennelong Program.

INFORMATION

- ☎ 9250 7111, box office 9250 7777
- 🚃🚢 Circular Quay
- 🚌 324, 325, 438, L38, Sydney Explorer
- ◷ box office Mon-Sat 9am-8.30pm, Sun 2½ hours before a performance
- Ⓢ free to the building; performance prices vary
- ⓘ tours ($12.90/8.90) every ½hr from 8.30am-5pm, backstage tours ($20.90) run when possible
- ⓔ vso@soh.nsw.gov.au; bookings@soh.nsw.gov.au; www.soh.nsw.gov.au
- ♿ excellent; ☎ 9250 7185 for info
- ✗ Bennelong, Concourse and Harbour restaurants, Cafe Mozart

Chris Mellor

DON'T MISS	• attending a performance • views from the forecourt • a guided tour, particularly a backstage tour

The Soap Opera House

The hullabaloo surrounding construction of the Sydney Opera House was an operatic blend of personal vision, long delays, bitter feuding, cost blowouts and narrow-minded politicking.

The NSW government held an international design competition in

1956, which was won by Danish designer Jørn Utzon, with plans for a $7 million building. Construction of Utzon's unique design began in 1959, but the project soon became a nightmare of cost overruns and construction difficulties. After political interference and disagreements with his consultants about construction methods, Utzon quit in disgust in 1966, leaving a consortium of 3 Australian architects to design a compromise interior. The parsimonious state government financed the eventual $102 million cost in true-blue Aussie fashion – through a series of lotteries.

After all the brawling and political bickering, the first public performance staged was, appropriately, Prokofiev's *War & Peace*. The preparations were a debacle and a possum appeared on stage during one of the dress rehearsals.

Things have gone relatively smoothly since, but, as with any performing arts house, the comedy hasn't always been scripted. A flustered Russian opera singer once missed his entrance because he was stuck in a lift and burst late onto the stage singing in Russian – the opera, unfortunately, was in Italian.

As well as the regular swag of high art, the Opera House has welcomed performers as diverse as kd lang, Ray Charles and Billy Connolly. It has hosted events as disparate as a Star Trek convention, a boot scooting dance-off, and the 1981 Mr Universe muscle-fest, in which Arnold Schwarzennegger out-bulged all comers.

After 25 years, the interior of the Opera House is due for a major refit and a happily unembittered Jørn Utzon has agreed to act as a consultant.

The inspiration for Utzon's creation is said to have evolved from his study of orange segments, palm fronds, shells or Mayan temples.

SYDNEY TOWER (3, K6)

The view from Sydney Tower's Observation Deck is the best city panorama in Australia and, at just over 300m, it's certainly the highest. On a clear day, the 360 degree views extend west to the Blue Mountains, south to Botany Bay and the airport, east across the length of the harbour to the heads and the Pacific Ocean, and down onto the streets of inner Sydney. It's a great way to get your bearings!

INFORMATION

- ✉ Centrepoint Shopping Mall, cnr Market & Pitt Sts
- ☎ 9229 7444
- 🚇 St James
- ⏱ 9am-10.30pm (till 11.30pm Sat)
- $ $10/4.50
- ⓘ free tours
- 🄴 www.centrepoint.com.au
- ♿ good
- ✕ Skylounge (snacks), Sydney Tower Restaurant

The shaft of the tower was designed to withstand earthquakes and freak wind speeds that are expected only once every 500 years. There's an enormous water tank at the top, above the observation deck, which acts as a stabilizer on very windy days. The lift to the top, which can carry up to 2000 people per hour, takes only 40 seconds to reach the observation level, which is 76 floors above the ground.

There are super-strength binoculars and free guided tours to help identify the most important sights, and photography has been assisted by the installation of anti-glare windows. The tower has a revolving restaurant and a sky-high cafe too; having an evening meal while rotating above the twinkling harbour city is unforgettable.

To find your way to the tower, enter the Centrepoint shopping mall from Market St and take the lift to the podium level, where you buy your ticket.

With all of Sydney at your feet it's not easy to decide where to go next.

TARONGA ZOO (2, E11)

A short ferry ride from Circular Quay, 30-hectare Taronga Zoo is one of the most spectacularly located zoos in the world. Its bushy hillside setting overlooks the harbour, meaning that many of its 4000 critters, including a substantial number of Australian ones, have million-dollar views. In a most un-Sydneylike display, they seem blissfully unaware of their privilege.

A zoo favourite is the **platypus habitat** in which day and night have been switched around so that the nocturnal platypussies are active during opening hours. There are plenty of photo opportunities in the koala display and the 'Australian Walkabout' lets you wander among kangaroos and wallabies who occasionally grace their human observers with a yawn. At **Discovery Farm**, kids (and adults) can get close to farm animals, and there's some good explanatory displays.

Taronga Zoo has an important endangered species breeding program, including Sumatran tigers, red pandas, orang-utans and snow leopards.

The zoo is on a steep hillside and it makes sense to work your way down if you plan to depart by ferry. If you can't be bothered walking to the top entrance, take a bus or the 'Aerial Safari' cable car.

Animals are generally more active in the early morning and late afternoon, especially on hot days. You're also likely to avoid most group visits if you visit at either end of the day.

INFORMATION

- ✉ Bradleys Head Rd, Mosman
- ☎ 9969 2777
- 🚌 247 (Spit Junction)
- ⛴ from Circular Quay
- 🕐 9am-5pm
- 💲 $16/8.50; a ZooPass ticket ($21/10.50), available at Circular Quay, includes return ferry rides to the zoo and admission fees
- ⓘ shows and keeper talks throughout the day, periodic twilight concerts; baby strollers available for hire
- 🌐 www.zoo.nsw.gov.au
- ♿ good, including access from the ferry stop; the zoo map clearly indicates accessibility
- 🍴 7 food outlets on-site, ranging from The Vines (kebab stand) to Treetops (à la carte licensed cafe)

Photo credits: Mike Cottee, Simon Bracken

All creatures great and small

DON'T MISS • giraffe enclosure with a view of the Harbour Bridge and Opera House • the Seal Show (1pm)

THE ROCKS   (3, E6)

The Rocks was the site of Sydney's first European settlement. Today, the area is unrecognisable from the squalid and overcrowded place it once was, when the sewers were open, the residents were raucous and the area was thronged with convicts, officers, whalers, sailors and street gangs.

Simon Bracken

INFORMATION

🚆🚌⛴ Circular Quay
ⓘ Visitors Centre, 106
  George St (☎ 9255
  1788, 1800 067676);
  walking tours
  ($12/8.50, children
  under 10 free) begin
  at 10.30am, 12.30 &
  2.30pm (weekdays)
  and 11.30am &
  2pm (weekends)
♿ difficult
✗ see page 83-4

The area fell into decline as modern shipping and storage facilities moved away from Circular Quay, and further declined following an outbreak of bubonic plague in 1900, which led to whole streets being razed. The construction of the Harbour Bridge 2 decades later resulted in further demolition.

The Rocks as we know it today was created by visionaries in the building industry and the union movement. Redevelopment has turned it into a sanitised, historical tourist precinct, full of narrow cobbled streets, fine colonial buildings, converted warehouses, tea rooms and stuffed koalas.

The oldest extant house in Sydney, built in 1816, is **Cadman's Cottage** (3, E6), 110 George St. It was once the home of the last government coxswain, John Cadman. When the cottage was built, it was on the waterfront, and the arches to the south of it housed longboats.

Susannah Place (3, E6), 58-64 Gloucester St, is a terrace of tiny houses dating from 1844. It's one of the few remaining examples of the modest housing which was once standard in the area. A site museum and old-time corner store are open on weekends (daily during January) from 10am-5pm.

The **Argyle Stores** (p. 60) on Argyle St was originally built as a bond store between 1826 and 1881; today it houses shops and studios.

A short walk west along Argyle St through the **Argyle Cut** (3, E5), an old tunnel excavated by convicts through the hill, takes you to the other side of the peninsula and **Millers Point** (3, E4), a delightful district of early colonial homes.

At the far end of the cut is **Garrison Church** (3, D5), the first church in Australia (1848). The church opens onto **Argyle Place**, an English-style village green on which any Australian has the right to graze livestock. Nearby, the human watering holes of the *Lord Nelson Brewery Hotel* (p. 89) on Kent St and the *Hero of Waterloo* on Windmill St (3, D5) vie for the title of Sydney's oldest pub. A short toddle towards the bridge, the **Colonial House Museum** (☎ 9247 6008; 10am-5pm; $1/50c), 53 Lower Fort St (3, D5), is a jumbled mishmash of artefacts giving an insight into how people lived in early Sydney.

Built in the 1850s, the **Sydney Observatory** (3, E5; ☎ 9217 0485) has a commanding position atop Observatory Hill overlooking Millers Point and the harbour. The observatory's museum (10am-5pm; free admission) has interesting interactive displays and videos on sky and space stuff. There are

Rock Bottom

Pub cellars in The Rocks were used as impromptu holding cells for the unruly (drunks were simply tipped down coal chutes to sleep off the grog) as well as hideouts for escaped convicts or crims on the run.

nightly skywatching shows ($8/3/18) at 6.15pm and 8.15pm (only one show in summer, at 8.30pm). Observatory Hill is one of Sydney's best picnic spots.

The **National Trust Centre** (3, F5; ☎ 9258 0123), in the old military hospital, houses the **SH Ervin Gallery** (p. 38) which has invariably rewarding exhibitions of Australian art.

The waterfront from Dawes Point (3, B6) to Darling Harbour was Sydney's busiest before container shipping and the construction of new port facilities at Botany Bay. Although Darling Harbour has been redeveloped, many wharves and warehouses around Dawes Point are still either mouldy or moulding. The **Wharf Theatre** (p. 95), at Pier Four, Hickson Rd, is home to the renowned Sydney Theatre and Sydney Dance companies. Volunteers host tours of the wharf ($5) – bookings are essential (☎ 9250 1700).

The site of the **public gallows**, in use until 1804, and Sydney's first jail are on Essex St (3, F5). The gallows were given a second lease of life (so to speak) from 1820 to 1840 while Darlinghurst Gaol was built.

Kids love the free puppet shows at The Rocks Puppet Cottage; ask for details at the Visitors Centre. The buskers and performers who hold court each weekend at The Rocks market (p. 62) are also fun.

Crafts, antiques and collectibles on offer at The Rocks weekend market.

VAUCLUSE HOUSE   (2, F13)

An imposing, turreted example of 19th century gothic Australiana, Vaucluse House (1828) is set in 10 hectares of lush gardens and grounds and is one of Sydney's finest old mansions. Decorated with beautiful period pieces from Europe, including Bohemian glass, Meissen china, and even a Venetian dining setting, the house offers visitors a rare glimpse into early, albeit privileged, colonial life in Sydney.

INFORMATION

- ✉ Wentworth Rd, Vaucluse
- ☎ 9388 7922
- 🚌 325 from Circular Quay
- ⏱ Tues-Sun 10am-4.30pm
- 💲 $6/3
- 𝒆 www.hht.nsw.gov.au
- ♿ ground floor only
- 🍴 Vaucluse House Tearooms (p. 84), Nielsen Park Kiosk (p. 85)

Simon Bracken

Vaucluse House was once owned by William Charles Wentworth, a famous early Australian who was outcast from high society because of his democratic leanings (Wentworth held the outrageous view that Australian-born colonials were the equals of the English). Wentworth is also famous for crossing the Blue Mountains in 1813 with Blaxland and Lawson, and writing the Australian constitution.

If in need of a swim, the Wentworth family would no doubt have wandered down to **Shark Beach** (p. 43) in Nielsen Park, once part of the Vaucluse House estate. Today it is one of the harbour's best family beaches, its waters protected from sharks by netting. As it is set inside the Sydney

Location, location, location – see how the other half lived at Vaucluse House.

Simon Bracken

Vaucluse House Tearooms is a pleasant spot to stop for tea and scones.

Harbour National Park, there are lovely scenic walks along the foreshore and some great views.

A desirable address even in the colony's early days, Vaucluse – today Sydney's most exclusive suburb – lies between Rose and Watsons bays, heading towards South Head. The abundance of wealth in Vaucluse makes it a good place to scope out interesting and ostentatious recent housing too. The houses at 48 Wentworth Rd and 25 Palmerston St are both worth a look: they were designed by Harry Seidler, an Austrian immigrant and Sydney's most visible architect.

Vaucluse House's rather grand stables (1829); now they house a small museum.

sights & activities

Most things to see and do in Sydney are in the city centre or nearby inner suburbs. Among the more interesting areas are the following.

Balmain (2, G8)

Once a tough, working-class neighbourhood with an active shipyard, Balmain attracted artists in the 1960s and renovators in the 1980s. Houses range from rumble-tumble terraces and mansions with dress-circle harbour views to the occasional veneer-clad abomination. The frangipani is pungent and the back streets so quiet that dogs still bother chasing every car.

Darling St, Balmain's spine, runs the length of the peninsula and is dotted with bookshops, restaurants, antique stores, bakeries and boutiques. There's a market (see page 62) every Saturday and myriad possibilities for a pleasant stroll.

Dr Balmain

As well as being the First Fleet surgeon renowned for removing a spear from the shoulder of Governor Arthur Phillip, Dr William Balmain was a rum importer and fiery character often involved in scrimmages and duels. The doctor was granted the land which is now Balmain in 1800 but was forced to transfer it to John Gilchrist, of Calcutta, India, a year later, probably after a rum deal went bad.

Bushy Balmain

Kangaroo hunts had stopped in Balmain around 1850, but in 1860 there was still enough wilderness for bushranger Captain Thunderbolt to escape from prison on nearby Cockatoo Island and disappear into 'the Balmain bush'.

For Poorer, then Richer

When Double Bay village was laid out in 1834, it was planned to be a good working class suburb. But in the 1860s, wealthier types began to build large houses there and the area was irredeemably fashionable from the 1870s.

Double Bay (2, H12)

If the runaround is a Range Rover, day wear is gym wear and hairdos grow three inches in the evenings, you're probably in the eastern 'burbs and you're quite likely in Double Pay, 'scuse me, *Bay*. This is a good place to scope out designer clothes for both adults and children, and there are plenty of cafes where you can catch your breath and sip a double-shot skinny soy latte.

Double Bay; double take

Double Bay's main shopping street is **Bay St**, which runs north off New South Head Rd. Bay St runs down to a quiet waterfront park and the ferry wharf. **Seven Shillings** beach and **Redleaf Pool** are both nice for a swim.

Glebe   (2, H8)

South-west of the city centre and close to the University of Sydney, Glebe has been ascending the social ladder in recent years, but it still has a bohemian atmosphere. The main thoroughfare, **Glebe Point Rd**, runs the length of the suburb from Broadway to Glebe Point and offers affordable restaurants, recycled clothing shops and second-hand bookshops.

The **Buddhist Temple**, on Edward St, was built by Chinese immigrants who arrived in Australia during the 1850s gold rush, and has been fully restored by Sydney's Chinese community. At the northern tip of Glebe Point Rd is **Jubilee Park**, with views across the bay to Rozelle and back towards the city.

Clergyman's Land

The word 'glebe' actually means 'land granted to a clergyman'. This particular glebe was assigned to Reverend Richard Johnson, the first chaplain of the colony. Though Johnson had convict helpers to clear the land and plant oranges and vegetables, most of Glebe stayed bushy and busy with parrots, kangaroos and swamp creatures until well into the 1830s.

Simon Bracken

'Mange bene' in Leichhardt – the little Italy of the inner-west.

Leichhardt   (2, H7)

In the early days of white settlement, Englishmen drove kangaroos from the Leichhardt scrub and shot at them on Balmain Point. These days, Leichhardt is known more for its gelati and cappuccinos than its wildlife. Italian immigrants settled here after WWII – often a husband would come first, then his wife and family would follow once housing and income were assured.

Norton St, which runs off Parramatta Rd, is now a bustling strip of Italian restaurants and the area has become increasingly popular with students, lesbians and young professionals.

Newtown   (2, J8)

When its residents started getting their noses pierced at salons instead of parties, it was obvious Newtown's heyday was over. Still, it hangs on as the inner west's counterculture centre, if a little self-consciously.

King St, the traffic-clogged aorta, is full of idiosyncratic shops and restaurants, many of them famously mediocre, but some of them damned good. You'll also find theatre, cinema, bands, thriving African and lesbian communities and so many yoga classes you'd think the whole of Sydney was looking through its third eye.

MUSEUMS & NOTABLE BUILDINGS

Anzac War Memorial

(3, M7) The interior dome of this memorial is studded with 120,000 stars, one for each New South Welsh man or woman who served in WWI. Pines nearby were grown from seeds gathered at Gallipoli in Turkey. There's a small museum downstairs.

✉ Hyde Park ☎ 9267 7668 🚇 Museum ⏰ 9am-5pm ⑤ free ♿ partial access

Name-A-Bug

The Australian Museum has a great 'search and discover' program. If you find a strange insect or hear a chilling howl, bring it in (or do your best impression) and scientists will identify it for you.

Australian Museum

(3, M8) A natural history museum with an excellent Australian wildlife collection and Aboriginal history gallery. There are guided tours on the hour and a special indigenous Australia tour at 2.30pm. Hands-on 'activity stations' are a favourite with kids.

✉ 6 College St ☎ 9320 6000 🅴 www. austmus.gov.au 🚇 Museum ⏰ 9.30am-5pm ⑤ $5/2/12 (special exhibitions extra) ♿ excellent

Australian National Maritime Museum

(3, J3) Find out about Australia's relationship with the sea, from Aboriginal canoes and the First Fleet to surf culture and the America's Cup. Vessels moored at the wharves include a naval destroyer, submerged submarine, racing yacht and Vietnamese refugee boat.

✉ Darling Harbour ☎ 9298 3777 🅴 www. anmm.gov.au 🚇 Town Hall, monorail, SLR 🚌 443 🚢 Darling Harbour ⏰ 9.30am-5pm (till 6pm Jan) ⑤ $10/6/25 ♿ good

Customs House

(3, F7) Recently restored, this wonderful building holds the Djamu Aboriginal Art Gallery (p. 39), the City Exhibition Space (with a 500:1 model of Sydney), the Object craft gallery, and excellent cafes and restaurants. Periodic performances are held in the soaring atrium.

✉ 31 Alfred St ☎ 9247 2285 🚇 🚌 🚢 Circular Quay ⏰ 9.30am-5pm ⑤ free (Djamu Gallery $8/5) ♿ excellent

Elizabeth Bay House

Simon Bracken

Elizabeth Bay House

(4, A6) When built in 1839, it was declared the finest dwelling in the colony. It's still breathtaking – if you stand in the oval salon and pretend you're master of the house, it's almost certain a maid will appear and call you for scones.

✉ 7 Onslow Ave, Elizabeth Bay ☎ 9356 3022 🅴 info@ho.hht. nsw.gov.au 🚇 Kings Cross 🚌 Sydney Explorer, 311 ⏰ Tues-Sun 10am-4.30pm ⑤ $6/3/15 ♿ ground floor only

Great Synagogue

(3, L7) This beautiful synagogue dates to 1878 and houses the longest-running congregation in Sydney. Particularly stunning is the ceiling with its gold leaf stars on a night-blue background.

✉ 166 Castlereagh St ☎ 9267 2477 🅴 info @greatsynagogue.org. au 🚇 Museum; St James ⏰ tours Tues & Thurs at noon; call for service times ⑤ free ♿ organise in advance

Hyde Park Barracks Museum

(3, K8) This Greenway-designed former convict quarters, immigration depot and women's asylum provides an interesting perspective of Sydney's social history.

✉ Queens Sq ☎ 9223 8922 🅴 www.hht.nsw. gov.au 🚇 St James ⏰ 9.30am-5pm ⑤ $6/3/15 (part of the display is free) ♿ ground floor only

Justice & Police Museum (3, F7)

Housed in the old Water Police Station, the museum has exhibits on various criminal activities – once a major industry in The Rocks nearby. A good place to see mugshots only a mother could love.

✉ **8 Phillip St (enter from Albert St)** ☎ **9252 1144** ◙ **info@ho.hht.nsw.gov.au; www.hht.nsw.gov.au** 🚊 🚌 🚢 **Circular Quay** ◷ **Sat-Sun 10am-5pm (Sat-Thurs in Jan)** ⑤ **$6/3** ♿ **ground floor only**

Museum of Sydney (3, G7)

This gossipy, tale-weaving museum uses installation art to explore Sydney's early history, with an emphasis on interactions between black and white Australians. Don't miss the Edge of the Trees sculpture in the forecourt where Koori and settler words whisper around you.

✉ **37 Phillip St** ☎ **9251 5988** ◙ **info@mos.nsw.gov.au; www.mos.nsw.gov.au** 🚊 🚌 🚢 **Circular Quay** ◷ **9.30am-5pm** ⑤ **$6/3/15** ♿ **excellent**

Parliament House (3, H8)

This is the world's oldest continuously operating parliament building – it's been in use since 1829. There are art exhibitions and a permanent display on the structure of government in NSW.

✉ **Macquarie St** ☎ **9230 2637** ◙ **www.parliament.nsw.gov.au** 🚊 **Martin Place** ◷ **9.30am-4pm** ⑤ **free** ♿ **excellent**

Powerhouse Museum (3, N3)

If you've ever wondered why the freezer door sticks, how lightning strikes, magnets grab or engines tick over, this is the place to get the lowdown. The superb displays emphasise interaction and education through experimentation, demonstration and fun, many of them geared specifically to children.

✉ **500 Harris St, Ultimo** ☎ **9217 0111** ◙ **www.phm.gov.au** 🚊 **SLR, monorail** 🚌 **888 from Circular Quay** 🚢 **to Darling Harbour** ◷ **10am-5pm** ⑤ **$8/2/18 – more for special exhibitions** ♿ **excellent**

St James Church (3, J7)

When construction of this Greenway and Macquarie co-production began it was to be a courthouse. Then the brief changed: make it a church! What is now the crypt was designed to be the court's holding cells. When completed in 1824, everyone from the governor to convicts attended the services.

✉ **Queens Sq** ☎ **9232 3022** ◙ **www.stjameschurchsydney.org.au** 🚊 **St James** 🚌 **Bondi Bay Explorer** ◷ **9am-5pm; tours by arrangement** ⑤ **free** ♿ **no**

St Mary's Cathedral (3, K8)

The first service was held here in 1833, but it wasn't until the eve of the 21st century that the spires of this massive Neogothic cathedral were finally completed. Neither of its pipe organs are loud enough to lead a lusty congregation in song so they are played simultaneously by 2 organ players linked by headphones.

✉ **cnr College St & St Marys Rd** ☎ **9220 0400** ◙ **www.syd.cath.org.au** 🚊 **St James** 🚌 **Bondi Bay Explorer** ◷ **daily; free tour on Sun at noon (after morning mass)** ⑤ **free** ♿ **good**

State Library of NSW (3, H8)

More a cultural centre than a traditional library, the collection includes Captain Cook's and Joseph Banks' journals and Captain Bligh's log. Of the more than 4 million items, the oldest is the prophecy of Isaiah written on vellum, and the smallest is a tablet-sized version of the Lord's Prayer. Excellent periodic exhibitions.

✉ **Macquarie St** ☎ **9273 1414** ◙ **library@slnsw.gov.au; www.slnsw.gov.au** 🚊 **Martin Place** ◷ **Mon-Fri 9am-9pm (exhibitions and shop till 5pm), Sat-Sun 11am-5pm** ⑤ **free** ♿ **excellent**

Mike Cottee

St Mary's soaring ceiling

Sydney Jewish Museum (4, E4)

Exhibits on Jews in general and in Australia in particular with a special focus on the Holocaust.

✉ 148 Darlinghurst Rd, Darlinghurst ☎ 9360 7999 ⊖ sydjmus@tmx. mhs.oz.au; www.sjm. com.au ⓠ Kings Cross 🚌 311, 389 ⊙ Mon-Thurs 10am-4pm, Fri 10am-2pm, Sun 11am-5pm (closed Jewish holidays) ⑤ $6/4/15 ⓥ no

Victoria Barracks

(4, H5) These Georgian buildings have been declared the finest in the British Empire. They've been in continuous use by the Australian Army since 1848. The museum here formerly served as a jail for long-term prisoners and soldiers on detention.

✉ cnr Oxford St & Greens Rd, Paddington ☎ 9339 3170 🚌 378, 380, 382, L82 ⊙ Thurs 10am-12.30pm (army band concert, guided tour, museum); Sun 10am-3pm (museum only) ⑤ free ⓥ good

SLIGHTLY FISHY

Oceanworld (2, B14)

This aquarium isn't as flashy as the one at Darling Harbour (which now owns it), but it's still great. There's shark feeding at 11.15am on Mon, Wed & Fri, and seal shows at 11.45am and 2pm daily, with an extra 3.30pm show on weekends.

✉ West Esplanade, Manly ☎ 9949 2644 ⓠ Circular Quay ⊙ 10am-5.30pm ⑤ $14.50/7.50-10/39, under 3s free ⓥ no

Sydney Aquarium

(3, K4) Displaying the richness, freakiness and downright scariness of Australian marine life, the aquarium's highlights are the 3 'oceanariums' moored in the harbour. Walk through underwater tunnels surrounded by slinky sharks and rays, Sydney Harbour marine life, or colourful fish and corals from the Great Barrier Reef. Informative displays accompany exhibits.

✉ Darling Harbour ☎ 9262 2300 ⊖ www. sydneyaquarium.com.au ⓠ Town Hall, monorail, SLR 🚌 888 from Circular Quay ⓠ Darling Harbour ⊙ 9am-10pm (last entry 9pm) ⑤ $17.50/8/39.90 ⓥ excellent

How They're Hooked

Sydney Aquarium's resident marine life is collected in various ways: they are caught using barbless hooks from Sydney Harbour or the nearby ocean, donated by people who come upon rare species, or acquired from other zoos and aquariums. Aquarium fish tend to live longer than their free-roaming counterparts as they have an assured food supply and are not placed in tanks with their natural predators.

Rum Hospital History

Sydney's **Parliament House** (p. 35) and **Mint** (3, J8) are housed in former wings of the infamous Rum Hospital, so-called because its builders were paid with a lucrative import monopoly on rum for 3 years, or 45,000 gallons. With its often appalling medical practices and lax treatment of patients, no-one was sad to see the hospital's main building razed and **Sydney Hospital** built on the site in 1894. Rubbing the snout of the Little Boar statue out front – and putting some coins in the donation box – is said to bring good luck.

GALLERIES

Sydney is flush with galleries, especially the inner eastern suburbs. The *Sydney Morning Herald's* 'Metro' section on Fridays lists galleries and art exhibitions, but for more detailed information get the monthly *Art Almanac* from galleries and newsagents. Note that many galleries take an extended break over Christmas and January.

PUBLIC GALLERIES

Art Gallery of NSW (3, J9)

One of the best public galleries in the country, the permanent displays of Australian, European, Asian and tribal art are definitely worth a visit. The Yiribana Gallery on Level 3 is the largest permanent display of Aboriginal and Islander art in Australia. Check the papers for the regular block-buster shows.

✉ Art Gallery Rd, the Domain ☎ 9225 1744 🅴 artmail@ag.nsw.gov.au; www.artgallery.nsw.gov.au 🚊 St James ⏲ 10am-5pm 🛈 permanent collection free, special exhibitions around $10 ♿ good

Museum of Contemporary Art (3, E6)

Since opening in November 1991, the MCA has provoked heated debate in the Sydney art world. Housed in a stately Art Deco building on Circular Quay, the museum's exhibits range from the heavily self-indulgent to the outstanding to the ridiculous. It also has an excellent – though rarely displayed – permanent collection.

✉ 140 George St, Circular Quay West ☎ 9241 5892 🅴 www.mca.com.au 🚌🚇🚢 Circular Quay ⏲ Wed-Mon 10am-5pm 🛈 $9/6/18 ♿ good

PRIVATE GALLERIES

Artspace

A spacious gallery featuring new works by local artists, including painting, video and sound installations.

✉ The Gunnery, 43-51 Cowper Wharf Rd, Woolloomooloo (4, A4) ☎ 9368 1899 🅴 artspace@artspace.org.au 🚉 Kings Cross 🚌 311 ⏲ Mon-Sat 11am-6pm 🛈 free except for special events ♿ good

Australian Galleries

Contemporary Australian painting and sculpture for the well moneyed and educated collector. The A-list of artists includes Davida Allen, Peter D Cole, Lloyd Rees and Margaret Olley.

✉ 15 Roylston St & 24 Glenmore Rd, Paddington (4, F8) ☎ 9360 5177 🚌 378, 380, 382, 390, L82 ⏲ Tues-Sun 10am-6pm ♿ good

Brett Whiteley Studio (4, K1)

This former studio of the notoriously fast-living Whiteley houses some of his best work. It would be hard to miss the apparent symbolism of the very large burnt match sculpture out front, matching the one at the Art Gallery of NSW.

✉ 2 Raper St, Surry Hills ☎ 9225 1740 🚌 Central 🚌 301-3, 343, 372, ⏲ Sat-Sun 10am-4pm 🛈 $6/4 ♿ yes

A visual feast awaits the culture vulture at the Art Gallery of NSW.

Queen St Fine Art

Before Woollahra gives itself over completely to antiques, there's a flurry of art galleries. This gallery is the best of the bunch.

✉ 34 Queen St, Woollahra (4, K9) ☎ 9363 3358 🚌 378, 380, 382, 389, L82 ⏰ Tues-Sat 11am-6pm, Sun 1-6pm Ⓢ free ♿ average

Ray Hughes Gallery

Ray Hughes is an art dealer in the old style: sell ice to Eskimoes could Ray. But the Australian, Aboriginal and Pacific region art he flogs is some of Australia's classiest. Plus it's all on display in the swishest warehouse you'll see this side of Manhattan.

✉ 270 Devonshire St, Surry Hills (4, K1) ☎ 9698 3200 🚇 Central ⏰ Tues-Sat 10am-6pm Ⓢ free ♿ no

Roslyn Oxley9 Gallery

The darlings of the art world reside here: Bill Henson, Dale Frank and Jenny Watson, among others. Roslyn's exhibitions during the Gay & Lesbian Mardi Gras are always a big hit.

✉ Soudan Lane (off 27 Hampden St), Paddington (4, G9) ☎ 9331 1919 📧 oxley9@roslyn oxley9.com.au 🚌 378, 380, 389, L82 ⏰ Tues-Fri 10am-6pm, Sat 11am-6pm Ⓢ free ♿ no

Sarah Cottier Gallery

Groovy gallery run by groovy people with groovy, sometimes comprehensible art. Run by the very young, oh-so-hip Sarah Cottier; definitely one for the Installation Set.

✉ 585 Elizabeth St, Redfern (2, J9) ☎ 9699 3633 🚇 Redfern; Central ⏰ Wed-Sat 11am-6pm Ⓢ free ♿ no

SH Ervin Gallery

Eclectic Australian art shows in the National Trust Centre. Cafe next door and (gasp) free parking on site.

✉ Observatory Hill, Watson Rd, The Rocks (3, F5) ☎ 9258 0123 🚌 339, 431-4 ⏰ Tues-Fri 11am-5pm, Sat-Sun 12-5pm Ⓢ $5/3 ♿ good

Sherman Galleries

Gene and Bill Sherman run a tight ship: they draw Australia's most successful artists to them like a magnet. Their 2 galleries, both in Paddington, are the slickest in Australia; that's because they sell more than anyone else.

✉ 16-18 Goodhope St (4, G6) and 1 Hargrave St (4, G8) ☎ 9331 1112, 9360 5566 🚌 389 ⏰ Tues-Sat 11am-6pm Ⓢ free ♿ excellent to Goodhope St, difficult to Hargrave St

Wagner Art Gallery

Old guard Aussie art – think Boyd, Nolan, Hart, Lindsay and Friend. Think big prices. Think champagne openings. Good for a quick look if you're in the area.

✉ 39 Gurner St, Paddington (4, G7) ☎ 9360 6069 🚌 389 ⏰ Mon-Sat 10.30am-6pm Ⓢ free ♿ partial access

Watters Gallery

A Sydney institution since 1964, Watters keeps pumping out quality: James Gleeson, Bob Klippel, Mike Brown, Richard Larter and Mambo's Reg Mombassa are just a few of the icons of Australian art they represent.

✉ 109 Riley St, East Sydney (4, D2) ☎ 9331 2556 🚌 389 ⏰ Tues & Sat 10am-5pm; Wed-Fri 10am-8pm Ⓢ free ♿ ground floor only

Yuill/Crowley Gallery

Conceptual work in all mediums, often controversial.

✉ The Block Suite 1, 8th fl, 428 George St (3, K6) ☎ 9223 1410 🚇 Town Hall; St James ⏰ Wed-Fri 11am-6pm (till 4.30pm Sat) Ⓢ free ♿ OK

Still life at the Australian Centre for Photography

Simon Bracken

PHOTOGRAPHIC GALLERIES

Australian Centre for Photography
For 25 years, ACP has exhibited the photographic gems of renowned local and international snappers. There is an excellent cafe on the premises.

✉ 257 Oxford St, Paddington (4, H7) ☎ 9332 1455 ✉ info@acp.au.com; www.acp.au.com 🚌 378, 380, 382, L82 ⏰ Tues-Sun 11am-6pm 💲 free ♿ good

Byron Mapp Gallery
Stylish photography from the iconic (Dupain/Mapplethorpe) to the newest and queerest – expect bodies galore. With on-site bookshop and espresso bar.

✉ 178 Oxford St, Paddington (4, H5) ☎ 9331 2926 ✉ gallery@wr.com.au; www.bias.net/byron-mappgallery 🚌 378, 380, 382, L82 ⏰ Mon-Sat 10am-5.30pm, Sun 1-5pm 💲 free ♿ OK

Stills Gallery
This former film studio is the backdrop for the exhibition and sale of Australia's best contemporary photography. Expect a wide spectrum of styles and media: photo-journalism, landscapes, digital imaging and photomontages.

✉ 36 Gosbell St, Paddington (4, E6) ☎ 9331 7775 ✉ photoart@stillsgallery.com.au; www.stillsgallery.com.au 🚌 378, 380, 382, L82 ⏰ Wed-Sat 11am-6pm 💲 free ♿ yes

ABORIGINAL ART

Djamu Gallery
Run by the Australian Museum, Djamu aims to stock Sydney's largest selection of books and catalogues relating to Aboriginal and Oceanic art and culture. There are hundreds of titles to peruse and a well chosen selection of artefacts from indigenous, Pacific island and Papua New Guinean communities.

✉ L2, Customs House, Alfred St (3, F7) ☎ 9320 6429 ✉ www.austmus.gov.au 🚌 🚌 ⛴ Circular Quay ⏰ 9.30am-5pm 💲 $8/5 ♿ excellent

Hogarth Galleries
Shows primarily Aboriginal artworks from Northern Australian communities. Their stock gallery and shop are complemented by a comprehensive exhibition program throughout the year.

✉ 7 Walker La, Paddington (4, G5) ☎ 9360 6839 🚌 378, 380, 382, L82 ⏰ Tues-Sat 11am-6pm 💲 free ♿ no

Thomas Thorpe Gallery
Housed in the original Paddington General Store, Thomas Thorpe gallery sells ethnographic, Asian, Pacific and contemporary Aboriginal artefacts. Collectors snap up fish totems and Neolithic jars while the rest of us peruse the shields, baskets, spears and shaman's bags.

✉ 2 Cascade St, Paddington (4, H8) ☎ 9331 8302 🚌 378, 380, 382, L82 ⏰ Tues-Sun 11am-6pm 💲 free ♿ yes

For Aboriginal gallery-shops, see page 65.

ANIMATION ART

The Cartoon Gallery
Mostly cel animation and limited edition animation artwork, with an emphasis on Japanese pieces.

✉ L2, Queen Victoria Bldg (3, K5) ☎ 9267 3022 ✉ cartoon@one.net.au; www.cartoongallery.com.au 🚌 Town Hall ⏰ Mon-Sat 10am-6pm (till 9pm Thurs), Sun 10am-5pm 💲 free ♿ yes

Silicon Pulp Animation Gallery
Devoted to animation stills, storyboards and design from painted cels to digital imaging.

✉ 176 Parramatta Rd, Stanmore (2, H7) ☎ 9560 9176 ✉ anigal@siliconpulp.com.au; www.siliconpulp.com.au 🚌 Stanmore 🚌 436-8, 440, 461, 480, 483 ⏰ Wed-Sat 11am-6pm 💲 free ♿ yes (call ahead)

Indigenous art is gaining increasing attention on the world stage.

Simon Bracken

QUIRKY SYDNEY

Drag Bag

'Walk in as a man, walk out as a woman,' claims Pencil, the owner of Drag Bag, a clothing and wig shop for drag queens. 'We've got cut'n'tuck underwear, waist cinchers and strappy stilettos in size 15. Plus there's make-up, diva-wear and very cheap, very glamorous wigs.'
✉ L1, 185 Oxford St, Darlinghurst (4, F2) ☎ 9380 8222 🚌 378, 380, 382, L82 ⏰ Mon-Sat 11am-6pm (till 5pm Sun)

Gashouse Refreshment Room

This local loungeroom style cafe opens according to the cycles of the moon. It's closed for 3 days over a full moon, 1 day for a new moon and for longer periods over summer and winter solstice. Regular customers get a passport with their photo attached. Everything is grilled, toasted, heated or poached and nothing is over $8. Bookings recommended.
✉ 37a Copeland St, Alexandria (2, J8) ☎ 9557 2589 🚉 Erskineville 🚌 355 ⏰ 9am-5pm (irregular) 👶 welcome ♿ yes

Goat Island (2, J5)

Goat Island has been a convict prison, shipyard, quarantine station and gunpowder depot. Today the island is used as the set of Water Rats, Australia's most popular TV cop show. Starry-eyed fans can take a special tour which takes in the sets and you might even see filming. Tours depart from Cadman's Cottage, 110 George St.
✉ Sydney Harbour, west of the Harbour Bridge ☎ 9247 5033 ⑤ $18/14 Heritage Tour (Mon, Fri, Sat-Sun), $18/14 Water Rats Tour (Wed), $22/18 Gruesome Tales Tour (Sat) ♿ OK

The Korean Bathhouse

This the perfect place to cleanse, detox, relax and be pampered. The basic rate includes wet and dry saunas, ginseng spa, hot and cold baths and a dozing room. Extras like massage, skin scrub, facial and shiatsu are reasonably priced.
✉ 1st fl, Hotel Capital, 111 Darlinghurst Rd, Kings Cross (4, C4) ☎ 9358 2755 🖥 www.citysearch.com.au/syd/koreanbaths 🚉 Kings Cross ⏰ Mon-Fri 10am-10pm, Sat-Sun 9am-10pm ⑤ $20 basic rate, more for extras ♿ OK

Sounds of Seduction at the Lansdowne Hotel

Sounds of Seduction combines sound, film and dance every which way. Think Japanese lounge music, a DJ dressed as an angel and dancers emerging from a film – it won't be that, but it will be just as out there.
✉ 2-6 City Rd, Chippendale (2, H9) ☎ 9211 2325 🚌 any bus down Broadway ⏰ Sat from 9pm ⑤ $5 ♿ no

Sweet Art

For the past 20 years, Sweet Art has been amazing Sydneysiders with detailed, imaginative and edible art works. The arresting window displays are a veritable feast of lifelike creations. Disney Studios, Elton John and kd lang are among the list of past customers.
✉ 96 Oxford St, Paddington (4, H5) ☎ 9361 6617 🚌 378, 380, 382, L82 ⏰ Mon-Sat 10am-6pm

Have your cake and gawk at it too!

Sydney Harbour Bridge Climb

It used to be bridge painters and outlaw daredevils who climbed the coathanger – now anyone with $100 and an adventurous spirit can do it. Bridge climbs take 3 hours, including an hour's preparation. Night climbs are available Thurs-Sat.
✉ 5 Cumberland St, The Rocks (3, D6) ☎ 9252 0077 🖥 admin@bridgeclimb.com; www.bridgeclimb.com ⏰ 7.45am-4.05pm (till 5.15pm Sat & Sun) ⑤ $98/79 (12-16 yrs); Sat-Sun $120/98 ♿ no

SYDNEY FOR CHILDREN

Many places put on extra activities for children during school holidays (December/January; 2-week breaks in April, July and September). A free monthly, *Sydney's Child*, lists activities and businesses geared to ankle-biters. Some of the following are outside the main central areas.

Kid's Branch, Royal Botanic Gardens

Educational theatre activities on the last Saturday of every month, suitable for 5-10 year olds. Theatre and puppetry programs run during school holidays.

✉ Education Centre, Royal Botanic Gardens (3, H9) ☎ 9231 8304 🚆 🚌 ⚓ Circular Quay ⑤ $10 ♿ advise in advance

Babysitters

The Wright Nanny (☎ 99297 341) supply first-aid qualified babysitters and nannies to the whole Sydney area. A casual nanny costs $13/hr plus a $15 agency fee. Babysitters are $10/hr plus a $15 agency fee.

Leuralla Toy & Model Railway Museum

Old toys and a working model railway. This is a looking-only museum.

✉ 36 Olympian Pde, Leura, Blue Mountains (1, B4) ☎ 4784 1169 ⏰ 10am-5pm ⑤ $6/2 ♿ OK

Manly Quarantine Station (2, D14)

The NPWS-run former Quarantine Station at North Head holds 2hr evening ghost tours for children, designed to inform, entertain and tap into kids' love of the spooky. Bookings essential.

✉ North Head Scenic Drive, Manly ☎ 9977 6522 ⚓ Manly, then bus 135 ⏰ Fri 6pm ⑤ $10 ♿ no

Oceanworld

See page 36.

Segaworld (3, M4)

Rides and games are divided into past (rollercoaster, ghost mobile), present (experiential film rides and a 'visionarium') and future (virtual reality spaceship rides, futuristic dodgem cars). Lose the kids or let your inner kid loose.

✉ Darling Harbour ☎ 9273 9273 🌐 www.segaworld.com.au 🚆 Town Hall, monorail, SLR 🚌 888 ⚓ Darling Harbour ⏰ Mon-Thurs 11am-8pm, Fri 11am-10pm, Sat 10am-10pm, Sun 10am-8pm ⑤ $28 for over 16s; $15-22 for under 16s ♿ good

Sunday Afternoon for Families, Art Gallery of NSW (3, J9)

Weekly family activity program, including dance, story-telling, magic acts, Aboriginal performance and exhibition-specific events.

✉ Art Gallery Rd, the Domain ☎ 9225 1744, 9225 1740 🌐 artmail@ag.nsw.gov.au; www.artgallery.nsw.gov.au 🚆 St James ⏰ Sun 2.30pm ⑤ free ♿ good; ☎ 9225 1775 to organise parking

Sydney Aquarium

See page 36.

Sydney Children's Museum

A science and technology playground for 3-10 year olds with a TV studio, computer games, human body models and more.

✉ cnr Pitt & Walpole Sts, Merrylands (next to Parramatta) (1, C8) ☎ 9897 1414 🚆 Merrylands ⏰ 10am-4pm ⑤ $5/5/18 ♿ partial access

The Rocks Puppet Cottage

Free puppet shows for children on weekends (more often during school holidays).

✉ Kendall Lane, The Rocks (3, E6) ☎ 9255 1788 🚆 🚌 ⚓ Circular Quay ⏰ Sat-Sun 11am, 12.30 & 2pm ⑤ free ♿ advise in advance

Wonderland

See page 52.

Segaworld – a real kid-magnet

Simon Bracken

BEACHES

Sydney's beaches are easily one of its greatest assets. They're popular on weekends but locals often take a dip before or after (or instead of) going to work. The beaches are easily accessible and usually clean, although some, like Balmoral, post warnings if stormwater runoff has made swimming inadvisable after heavy rains.

Nude is Rude

Daylight bathing was banned in Sydney until 1903 when sweltering Manly officials braved scandal and lifted the injunction. In 1907, a law was passed prescribing neck-to-knee swimming costumes; beach inspectors even patrolled the strands with tape measures.

By 1930 though, the creep was on and it was only a matter of time before nude was no longer rude.

There are 2 types of beaches – harbour beaches, which are sheltered, calm and usually smaller, and ocean beaches, which often have good surf.

Swimming is generally safe, but at the ocean beaches you should only swim within the red-and-yellow flagged areas, which are patrolled by the famed lifesavers. There are some notorious rips even at Sydney's most popular beaches, so don't underestimate the surf just because it doesn't look threatening. Efforts are made to keep the surfers separate from the swimmers. If you're around during summer, try to catch a surf lifesaving competition – they're very entertaining.

Shark patrols operate during the summer, and beaches are often netted – Sydney has only had one fatal shark attack since 1937 and shark sightings are rare enough to make the news. Many of Sydney's beaches are 'topless' and a couple are nude: do as the locals do.

Catching some rays at Shark Bay; but don't forget the sunscreen.

Ross Barnett

Avalon (1, A10)
A perfect beach with orangey sand – just try to pretend you don't want to live there.
🚌 L88, L90, 190 to northern beach ✕ Swell (snacks), Cafe Turtles (Mediterranean, outdoor dining)

Balmoral (2, D12)
A sheltered beach popular with North Shore familes. There's a grassy area for picnics and theatre by the sea in summer.
🚌 257 from Spit Junction, 238 from Taronga Zoo ✕ Awaba (p. 74), Bottom of the Harbour (much lauded fish & chips)

Bondi
See page 14.

Bronte (2, J13)
A superb family-oriented beach hemmed in by a bowl-shaped park and sandstone headlands.
🚌 378 to southern beach ✕ Sejuiced

Camp Cove, Watsons Bay (2, E14)
This is where Arthur Phillip first landed in Sydney but today's families and topless bathers don't dwell on it.
🚌 324, 325 to harbour beach ✕ bring a picnic

Clovelly (2, K13)
A breakwater has turned this U-shaped bay into more of a pool. A wheelchair ramp goes right into the water and there's a decent walk-in scuba dive.
🚌 339, 341 to southern beach ✕ Jilted Anchovy (pasta and pizza), Clovelly pub (friendly local scene)

Collaroy (1, B9)
This beach stretches for 2 suburbs – room enough for families, fishers, surfers and ray-soakers.
🚌 155, 157, 182, 184, 189, 190 to northern beach ✕ Silverado's beachside

Coogee (2, K13)
The name 'coogee' comes from the Aboriginal word for bad smell or rotting seaweed, but don't be put off – what you'll find is a wide, sweeping beach full of frisbees, backpackers, surfers and groovers in black bathers reading Kafka.
🚌 372, 373, Airport bus 351 to southern beach ✕ beach cafe

Cronulla
See page 45.

Dee Why (1, B9)
Grommets hit the surf and mums hit the pool at this family-oriented beach.
🚌 136 to northern beach ✕ Stella Blu (Italian), The Thai & I

Lady Bay, South Head (2, E14)
Also known as Lady Jane beach, this is Sydney's most accessible nude beach; it's also gay-friendly.
🚌 324, 325 to harbour beach ✕ bring a picnic

Manly
See page 51.

Palm Beach (1, A9)
Golden sand, stars and starspotters, nudists at the northern end, and Pittwater sailing just round the peninsula – kinda heavenly.
🚌 190 to northern beach ✕ North Palmy Kiosk, Beachcomber

Flick a flipper at Lady Bay.

(sandwiches, ice creams, chips), Boardwalk (restaurant/bar)

Shark Beach, Vaucluse (2, F13)
A shark net actually protects this beach so there's no need to think of *Jaws*; its a family scene, with great views and a shady adjoining park.
🚌 325 to harbour beach ✕ Nielsen Park Kiosk

Tamarama
(2, J13) A pretty cove with strong surf and a reputation for buff bodies.
🚌 361, 380 to southern beach ✕ beach cafe

No Thanks, Pamela
The most popular show in the world, *Baywatch*, filmed an episode at Avalon Beach but the producers' attempt to relocate the show there was scuttled by local residents who feared a silicon leakage would pollute Avalon's pristine waters. The show ended up in Hawaii.

OFF THE BEATEN TRACK

Abbotsford   (2, F5)

If the day screams 'foreshore! picnic!' but holds a 'no crowds' card, you might consider heading for Abbotsford, a ferry ride west of Circular Quay along the Parramatta River. It's possible to make this a full day excursion as there's a 16km path which circles the whole Abbotsford/Drummoyne peninsula, hugging the bays and then cutting back across Fivedock Park. Of course, you can save your shoe leather and head straight for **Quarantine Reserve** or **Henry Lawson Park**, both lovely for a picnic. The parks and the foreshore walk are both wheelchair accessible.

Peaceful afternoon at Castle Rock Beach

Castle Rock   (2, C12)

Castle Rock beach is about 6.5km (2½hrs) walk from Manly Cove along the Manly Scenic Walkway (p. 51). It's a superscenic beach staked out mostly by locals, who walk down the stairs from Ogilvy Rd, Balgowlah. This is perfect picnic territory and the rockpools are worth exploring; kids find it fascinating. Be warned that the nearest toilets are about 15mins walk further west at Clontarf beach.

Cronulla (1, D9)

Looong sandy beaches, dependable surf, teen scenes and burger joints: Cronulla is about as far south as you can get and still be in Sydney. It's an unpretentious local hangout, where you'll see kids doing surf lifesaving training, parents sunning themselves and lots of people board-riding. Up on the esplanade there's a slew of fish & chip shops (Cronulla is known for its oysters) and a flurry of waterfront apartments but the Returned & Services League (RSL) club is still the best looking structure.

A ferry crosses Port Hacking, south of Cronulla, and travels to Bundeena, the gateway to the **Royal National Park** where there are some excellent short walks. The walk east to Jibbon beach is especially lovely; you pass Aboriginal rock paintings on the way.

To get to Cronulla catch a CityRail train from Central station; they run every half-hour.

Hunters Hill (2, E6)

The elegant village-like suburbs of Hunters Hill and Woolwich (2, E7) are on a spit at the junction of the Parramatta and Lane Cove rivers. Many of the sandstone houses here were built by immigrant French and Italian stonemasons between 1850 and 1900. The National Trust-operated **Vienna Cottage** (☎ 9258 0123), 38 Alexandra St, Hunters Hill, is a stone cottage built in 1871 by Jacob Hellman; it is typical of the era. It's open on the 2nd and 4th Sunday of the month from 11am-4pm. Entry is $2.

The ferry trip from Circular Quay to Hunters Hill and Woolwich (Valentia St wharf) is an attraction in itself, offering fabulous views both upriver and across the harbour. It makes sense to catch bus 358 from the pier to Alexandra St, where there are cafes and shops to peruse, and then wind your way back down to the pier.

Take a ferry to get away from it all.

McMahons Point (2, F9)

This pleasant, sleepy suburb on the North Shore is tipped by **Blues Point Reserve**, named after the Jamaican-born Billy Blue, who ferried people across from Dawes Point in the 1830s. Blues Point Tower, designed by architect Harry Seidler, was one of the first high-rise buildings on the harbour.

To get there, catch a ferry from Circular Quay, or cross the Harbour Bridge and walk west around the headland.

KEEPING FIT

Sydney's sunshine, parks and can-do attitude add up to plenty of ways to get the heart rate up. There have long been deals crunched over a game of tennis and scripts written while pounding the pool. And since the city scored the Olympics, every jogger makes out as though they're training for the big one.

Golf

Golf is very popular in Sydney – there are over 80 courses in the metropolitan area. That said, about half of them are private. Book ahead to play on the public courses, particularly on weekends, or use whatever connections you have to get onto the private greens.

Gyms

Most of the larger hotels have a gym and a pool available for guests; many make these facilities available to visitors for a fee. Otherwise, there are plenty of independent gyms around town which have special rates for casual visits.

Sailing & Boating

There are plenty of sailing schools, yacht clubs and boat charter companies in Sydney. The Cruising Yacht Club of Australia (☎ 9363 9731; www.cyca.com.au) can help with general enquiries; see the *Yellow Pages* for schools and charters.

Pittwater and Broken Bay offer some of the world's best sailing.

Surfing

South of the Heads, the best spots are Bondi, Tamarama, Coogee and Maroubra. Cronulla, south of Botany Bay, is also a serious surfing spot. On the North Shore, there are a dozen surf beaches between Manly and Palm Beach.

Surfboards, boogie-boards and wetsuits can easily be hired from shops near the popular surf beaches. Prices for a board and suit start at around $20 for 3hrs.

Swimming

Sydney's harbour beaches offer sheltered water conducive to swimming. Nothing beats being knocked around in the waves which pound the ocean beaches; however, make sure to follow lifeguard instructions and swim between the red-and-yellow flags.

There are more than 100 public swimming pools in Sydney, some of them beautifully set into the beach.

Tennis

There are thousands of tennis courts in Sydney open to the public. Tennis NSW (☎ 9331 4144; www.tennisnsw.com.au) provides information.

Andrew 'Boy' Charlton Swimming Pool

Set on the edge of the Royal Botanic Gardens, this 50m outdoor pool overlooks Woolloomooloo Bay.
✉ the Domain, Woolloomooloo Bay ☎ 9358 6686 🚢 🚌 🛥 Circular Quay ⏰ Sat-Thurs 6.30am-8pm, Fri 6.30am-7pm (closed during winter) 💲 $2.50

Barnwell Park (2, G4)

Public golf course, 18 hole par-61, quite flat; pull-buggies and gear available for hire.
✉ cnr William St & Lyons Rd, Five Dock ☎ 9713 9019 🚌 L38 or 461 from Central ⏰ dawn to dusk 💲 $10/14 for 9/18 holes; weekends $16/12

Bondi Golf Course

(2, H14) This public golf course is an 18 hole par-56 affair; club hire available.
✉ Military Rd, North Bondi ☎ 9130 3170 (clubhouse), 9130 1981 (pro shop) 🚌 380, 389 to North Bondi terminal ⏰ Mon-Fri 7am-dusk, Sat-Sun 12.30pm-dusk 💲 $12 for 9 holes

City Gym

Open virtually 24 hours, this gym has all the standard work-out equipment, plus a steam room, yoga and various aerobics classes.
✉ 107 Crown St, Darlinghurst (4, C2) ☎ 9360 6247 🚌 Kings Cross; Museum ⏰ Mon 5am till Sat 10pm, Sun 8am-10pm 💲 $10-12

King George VI Memorial Pool

Heated 50m outdoor pool with 8 lanes, plus a gym.
✉ Victoria Park, Chippendale (2, H9) ☎ 9660 4181 🚌 any down Broadway/Parramatta Rd ⏰ Mon-Fri 6am-7.15pm, Sat-Sun 7am-5.45pm 💲 pool $2.50; gym $5

Moore Park (2, J10)

Old, established inner-city public golf course, 18 hole par-70, with a pro-shop and electric carts and clubs for hire. Booking recommended, especially on weekends.
✉ cnr Cleveland St & Anzac Pde, Moore Park ☎ 9663 3960 🚌 any down Anzac Pde ⏰ dawn to dusk (driving range closes 10pm) 💲 $24 for 18 holes, $27 on weekends

North Sydney Olympic Pool

Superbly located next to Luna Park at the northern end of the Sydney Harbour Bridge, this heated 50m outdoor pool has 9 lanes. By the time you read this a 25m indoor pool, spa, gym, sauna and restaurant should have been added to the site.
✉ Milsons Point (3, A7) ☎ 9955 2309 🚌 Milsons Point 🛥 Milsons Point Wharf ⏰ Mon-Fri 5.30am-9pm; Sat-Sun 5.30am-7pm 💲 $3

Prince Alfred Park Pool

Outdoor, unheated 50m pool close to Central station.
✉ Chalmers St, Surry Hills (2, H10) ☎ 9319 7045 🚌 Central ⏰ 6.30am-8pm (closed during winter) 💲 $2.50

Sydney International Aquatic Centre

Feel like an Olympian in the state-of-the-art aquatic centre at Homebush. Apart from the pool built for the 2000 Games, there's also a gym, spa, sauna and all manner of fitness classes.
✉ Olympic Blvd, Homebush Bay (2, F1) ☎ 9752 3666 🚌 Olympic Park 🚌 401 or 403 from Strathfield to Olympic Park ⏰ Mon-Fri 5am-10pm, Sat-Sun 6am-8pm 💲 gym $12; pool $5

On the high seas – Sydney offers some world-class sailing opportunities.

out & about

WALKING TOURS
Hyde Park to the Harbour

Start at the south-western tip of Hyde Park **(1)**, stroll past the Anzac War Memorial **(2)**, stop in at the Australian Museum **(3)** on College St and then head back through the gardens to the wonderful Archibald Fountain **(4)**. Cut east to St Mary's Cathedral **(5)**, then take St James Rd to Macquarie St, where a parade of beautiful public buildings awaits.

First there's Hyde Park Barracks **(6)** and, opposite, St James Church **(7)**. If the belly hollers, grab a sandwich at *Caruthers* **(8)** next door, then continue to The Mint **(9)** and Sydney Hospital **(10)**, where you can rub the snout of the *Little Boar* statue out front for good luck. Parliament House **(11)** and the State Library **(12)** are next along; from there, cut through the Royal Botanic Gardens **(13)**, up past the Conservatorium of Music **(14)**, and continue north along Macquarie St to the Opera House **(15)**.

Take the Circular Quay East walkway to Alfred St and Customs House **(16)** and continue on to the Museum of Contemporary Art **(17)**. Its *MCA Cafe* is a good place to stop for another bite, before heading on to George St and The Rocks **(18)**. When you're done, head back to Circular Quay for onward transport.

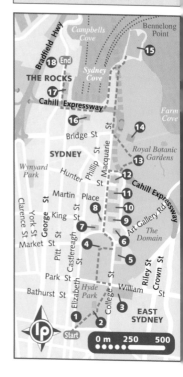

distance 3km **duration** 2hrs
start 🚇 Museum
end 🚇 🚌 🚢 Circular Quay

SIGHTS & HIGHLIGHTS

Anzac War Memorial (p. 34)
Australian Museum (p. 34)
St Mary's Cathedral (p. 35)
Hyde Park Barracks Museum (p. 34)
St James Church (p. 35)
The Mint & Sydney Hospital (p. 36)
Parliament House (p. 35)
State Library of NSW (p. 35)
Royal Botanic Gardens (p. 20)
Opera House (p. 24)
Customs House (p. 34)
Museum of Contemporary Art (p. 37)
The Rocks (p. 28-9)

Playing with the Big Boys

Giant kings, queens and subjects come out for chess games held under the trees at the northern end of Hyde Park, on weekdays from 11.30am-2.15pm. Stand and watch, or challenge someone to a friendly game.

Paddo Pavement Pound

Begin at Victoria Barracks **(1)**, then head up Oxford St to Glenmore Rd, where you can stop in at Australian Galleries **(2)** and Barry Stern Galleries **(3)**. Turn into Gipps St and, at the Prospect St corner, you'll find Paddington's oldest terraces **(4)**, built in the 1840s for quarrymen and stonemasons working on the barracks.

Turn left at Shadforth St, which bends into Liverpool St, and Hogarth Galleries **(5)** is to your right. Continue up Liverpool St and turn right into Glenmore Rd. Follow it along a few hundred metres to Five Ways **(6)**, the old civic centre of the suburb. The *Royal Hotel*, which dominates the intersection, is a good place to get a cleansing ale or some lunch.

After Glenmore Rd becomes Gurner St you'll come to Wagner Art Gallery **(7)** and, a bit further, there's a great view of Ruchcutters Bay at the Cambridge/Norfolk St intersection **(8)**. Turn right at Cascade St, right again at Paddington St, then head left down William St, where there are eclectic boutique shops **(9)**. When you hit Oxford St, turn left for Paddington Bazaar **(10)** if it's a Saturday, or rest your pavement pounders at *Hot Gossip Cafe* **(11)** or Centennial Park **(12)**.

SIGHTS & HIGHLIGHTS

Victoria Barracks (p. 36)
Australian Galleries (p. 37)
Paddington's oldest terrace houses
(p. 19 for more on Paddington)
Hogarth Galleries (p. 39)
Wagner Art Gallery (p. 38)
Paddington Bazaar (p. 62)
Centennial Park (p. 19)

Wall-to-wall terraces line Paddo's streets.

distance 2.5km **duration** 2hrs
start 🚌 378, 380, 382, L82
end 🚌 378, 380, 382, L82

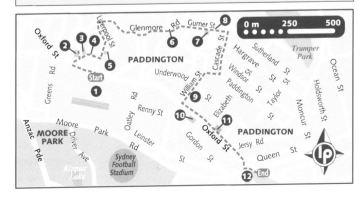

Innerwest Waterside Wander

Start your wander at Darling Harbour **(1)** where you might like to visit the aquarium, one of the museums or lighten your wallet at Star City casino. From the western end of Pyrmont Bridge **(2)**, follow the road along to the Sydney Fish Market **(3)** on Blackwattle Bay, where you can admire the catch and the views. From here take Bridge Rd past Wentworth Park **(4)**, where there's greyhound racing, then turn right onto Burton St.

At the end of Burton St some steps lead up to Ferry Rd – once there turn right and head to *The Boathouse on Blackwattle Bay* **(5)**, one of Sydney's most innovative seafood restaurants, for a meal. Then head back up Ferry Rd until you reach Glebe Point Rd, where you can while away an hour or two checking out the terraces, trendy shops and cafes.

SIGHTS & HIGHLIGHTS

Darling Harbour (p. 16)
Sydney Fish Market (p. 71)
Wentworth Park (p. 100)
The Boathouse on Blackwattle Bay (p. 79)
Glebe Point Rd (p. 33)
Blackwattle Canteen (p. 86)
Glebe Market (p. 62)

distance 6km **duration** 3hrs
start Darling Harbour
end Broadway 431-4

At the northernmost end of the street is Jubilee Park **(6)**, with its great views across Rozelle Bay, and the *Blackwattle Canteen* **(7)**, a tasty stopover for coffee and cake. The street's southern end is home to Glebe Market **(8)** every Saturday – from there it's a quick stroll south to Broadway where buses will take you back to the city.

A spot of lunch at Blackwattle Canteen

Simon Bracken

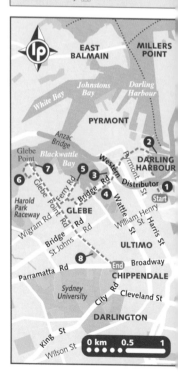

Manly Scenic Walkway

This gorgeous and memorable walk follows the harbour shore west from Manly Cove **(1)** through Fairlight, Balgowlah, Balgowlah Heights and Clontarf on Middle Harbour. Parts of the walk go through Sydney Harbour National Park but mostly the path winds between residential areas and the water.

Points of interest from the Manly end include: Fairlight **(2)**, Forty Baskets **(3)** and Reef beaches **(4)** (the latter, a nude beach, involves a slight detour from the main track); great views south of Dobroyd Head **(5)**; and ancient Aboriginal rock carvings **(6)** on a sandstone platform between the Cutler Rd Lookout and Grotto Point **(7)**. Though there's a good chance you'll come upon other tourists and their zoom lenses, the walkway is also popular with locals powerwalking, jogging and giving Fido his constitutional.

There's not much in the way of eating establishments en route but you can fortify yourself at Manly Cove before you head out and there are picnic tables at North Harbour Reserve, Tania Park and Clontarf beach **(8)**. The walkway ends at The Spit Bridge **(9)**, where you can catch a bus back to the city.

SIGHTS & HIGHLIGHTS

Manly Cove
Fairlight Beach
Forty Baskets Beach
Reef Beach
Dobroyd Head
Aboriginal rock carvings
Grotto Point
Clontarf Beach
The Spit Bridge

Duke of Hazard

Prince Alfred, Duke of Edinburgh, survived an assassination attempt at Clontarf beach in 1868. Though the bullet gave him a good whang, Alfie's sturdy indian rubber braces absorbed much of the impact and he lived to be princely some more.

distance 10km **duration** 4hrs
start 🚶 Manly Cove
end Spit Bridge 🚌 169 to/from Wynyard train station

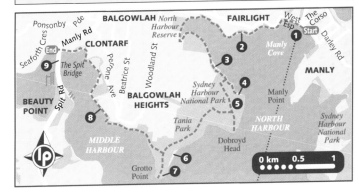

EXCURSIONS
Ku-ring-gai Chase National Park   (1, A9)

Simon Bracken

This 18,000 hectare park, 24km north of the city centre, has that classic Sydney mixture of sandstone, bushland and water vistas, plus walking tracks, horseriding trails, picnic areas and Aboriginal rock engravings. Plan on a full day.

Elevated parts of the park offer superb **views** across the surrounding inlets, and you may see **lyrebirds** at West Head during the May-July mating period. The best places to see **Aboriginal engravings** are on the Basin Track and Garigal Aboriginal Heritage Walk.

It's unwise to swim in Broken Bay because of sharks, but there are safe netted swimming areas at Illawong Bay and the Basin.

Wildlife Parks

In addition to the large national parks on the fringes of Sydney, there are several places in the outer suburbs where you can see native animals – often at close range.

Popular **Waratah Park**, 30km north of Sydney on the edge of Ku-ring-gai park, is a good place to see native fauna. The TV series *Skippy* was filmed here in the 60s. There's koala petting from 11am-4pm. Dalmyles run half-day tours from Circular Quay at 8.30am daily (☎ 9977 5567; $54/49).

The **Australian Wildlife Park,** located at **Wonderland** theme park, 38km north-west of Sydney, houses all sorts of native animals. The theme park has Aussie enactments (gold rush, woolshed), rides, pools, water slides and the incongruous Hanna-Barbera Land.

Parramatta   (1, B8)

Parramatta, 24km west of Sydney, was the second European settlement in Australia. When Sydney proved a very poor area for farming, Parramatta was selected in 1788 as the site of the first farm community. Today, it has merged with Sydney's sprawling western suburbs.

Despite the sometimes insensitive manner in which Parramatta has been modernised over the years, it retains a hint of country-town atmosphere and some beautiful, unique historic buildings. Plan on spending a whole day exploring it.

Old Government House (☎ 9635 8149) in Parramatta Park dates from 1799 and is built on the site of the colony's first farm. Originally a country retreat for the early rulers, it is now a museum (Mon-Fri 10am-4pm, Sat-Sun 11am-4pm; $6/4/12; ♿ no).

The oldest surviving European home in Australia, **Elizabeth Farm** (☎ 9635 9488; www.hht.nsw.gov.au/fmuseums.html) at 70 Alice St, Rosehill, was built in 1793 by John and Elizabeth Macarthur, whose experiments with sheep-breeding formed the basis of Australia's wool industry.

John Macarthur also controlled the lucrative rum trade and engineered the removal of several governors who tried to control him. The house is classic old colonial with broad verandas, a traditional garden and reproduction colonial furniture and fittings (10am-5pm; $6/3/15; ♿ excellent).

Built for the Macarthurs' daughters' governess in 1824, **Hambledon Cottage** (☎ 9635 6924) on Hassall St was used as a weekend lodging until Penelope Lucas, one of few women in the colony, moved there when she retired (Wed, Thurs, Sat & Sun 11am-4pm; $3/2.50; ♿ yes).

Experiment Farm Cottage (☎ 9635 5655), 9 Ruse St, is a fine example of a homestead built in 1820 and furnished in 1840s style. Its curious name comes from an experiment in trust: Governor Phillip named the grant when he handed it over to convict farmer James Ruse in 1791 (Tues-Thurs 10am-4pm, Sun 11am-4pm; $6/4; ♿ no).

The **Royal NSW Lancers Barracks** (☎ 9635 7822), on the corner of Station, Smith & Darcy Sts, house Australia's oldest regiment (1828), with more battle honours than any other in Australia. There are several historic buildings inside and a museum in 1828-era Linden House (Sun 10am-4pm; $2/50c; ♿ no).

Windsor & Richmond (1, A6)

On the banks of the Hawkesbury River, 55km north-west of Sydney, **Windsor** has many fine old colonial buildings, such as the **Hawkesbury Museum** (☎ 4577 2310; 10am-4pm; $2.50/1.50; ৬ no), in the same building as the information centre. Other old buildings include the convict-built **St Matthew's Church** (1820), designed, like the old **courthouse** (1822), by convict architect Francis Greenway.

George St has more historic buildings, and the **Macquarie Arms Hotel** is reckoned by some to be the oldest pub in Australia. It's a good place to stop for lunch.

INFORMATION

ⓘ Windsor Information Centre, Daniel O'Connell Inn, Thompson Sq (☎ 4577 2310); National Parks & Wildlife Service in Richmond, 370 Windsor St (☎ 4588 5247)

🚆 CityRail to Windsor and Richmond from Central

🚌 M2 to Windsor Rd (Route 40)

Richmond is 6km west of Windsor, at the end of the CityRail line and at the start of the Bells Line of Road across the Blue Mountains.

The town dates from 1810 and has some fine Georgian and Victorian buildings. These include the **courthouse** and **police station**, on Windsor St, and, around the corner on Market St, **St Andrew's Church** (1845).

Plan on spending a full day to see the neighbouring towns.

Echo Point, Katoomba, provides striking views of The Three Sisters rock formation.

Ross Barnett

Katoomba (1, B4)

Katoomba, 110km west of Sydney, and the adjacent towns of **Wentworth Falls** and **Leura,** form the tourist centre of the Blue Mountains. It makes for a great day out and it is worth overnighting. Katoomba is where the Sydney 'plains-dwellers' escape the summer heat, and it has a long tradition of catering to visitors.

Despite the number of tourists and its proximity to Sydney, Katoomba has an uncanny ambience of another time and place, an atmosphere accentuated by its Art Deco and Art Nouveau guesthouses and cafes, its thick mists and occasional snowfalls.

The main attraction is **Echo Point**, near the southern end of Katoomba St, about 1km from the shopping centre. Here are some of the best views of the Jamison Valley and the magnificent **Three Sisters** rock formation.

West of Echo Point, at the junction of Cliff Drive and Violet St, are the **Scenic Railway** and **Scenic Skyway** (☎ 4782 2699; $5/2). The railway was built in the 1880s to transport coal miners; its 45° incline is one of the steepest in the world. The Scenic Skyway cable car travels some 200m above the valley floor, traversing Katoomba Falls gorge.

The **Explorers Tree**, just west of Katoomba near the Great Western Highway, was marked by Blaxland, Wentworth and Lawson, who, in 1813, were the first Europeans to find a way over the mountains.

The 12km-return bushwalk to the **Ruined Castle** rock formation on Narrow Neck Plateau, dividing the Jamison and Megalong valleys another couple of kilometres west, is one of the best – watch out for leeches after rain. The **Golden Stairs** lead down from this plateau to more bushwalking tracks.

The house of Norman Lindsay, acclaimed Australian artist and *bon vivant*, is at **Faulconbridge** (☎ 4751 1067). This was also the setting of the silly film *Sirens*, starring Elle Macpherson.

The National Parks & Wildlife Service organises various tours; check with the Visitors Centre in Echo Point. During the Spring and Autumn Garden festivals, locals open their gardens to visitors.

INFORMATION

- ⓘ Blue Mountain Tourism Authority (☎ 1800 641 227, 1300 653 408; *e* www.bluemountain tourism.org.au); Visitors Centre, Echo Point (9am-5pm)
- 🚆 CityRail from Central (hourly)
- 🚗 Parramatta Rd west from the city centre, and detour onto the Western Motorway (M4) at Strathfield (it becomes the Great Western Hwy west of Penrith)
- ✕ Savoy, Blues Cafe, Paragon Cafe, Chork Dee, Avalon Restaurant
- 🛏 Hydro Majestic Hotel (☎ 4788 1002), Lilianfels Blue Mountains (☎ 4780 1200)

Ross Barnett

Kangaroos are commonly sighted in the bush.

ORGANISED TOURS

There's a vast array of city and surrounds tours to choose from. Companies offer everything from koala-cuddling in the Blue Mountains, wine tippling in the Hunter Valley, Sydney Harbour swooping in a seaplane, to getting down and dirty in the bush. Most tours offer hotel pick-up and also swing by Circular Quay.

BLUE MOUNTAINS
Gray Line
This full-day tour takes in Katoomba, the Three Sisters, Echo Point and a wildlife park on the way back.
☎ 9241 3983
⑤ $83/41.50

BUSH TOUR
Footloose
Five day, guided 'gourmet walker' adventures, mixing epicurean delights with glorious bush and water scenery. Combine national park and foreshore walks, ferry trips and visits to Palm Beach with dinners at top-class restaurants.
☎ 9979 8775 ❸ info@footloose.com.au
⑤ $824 for 5 days/4 nights, all inclusive

HARBOUR CRUISES
Captain Cook Cruises
A hop-on, hop-off service that stops at the Opera House, Watsons Bay, Taronga Zoo and Darling Harbour. Boats run every 2hrs from 9.30am-3.30pm.
✉ Wharf 6, Circular Quay (3, E7) ☎ 9206 1111
⑤ $20/12-15

Goat Island
See page 40.

Matilda & Sail Venture Cruises
A variety of sailing and cruising, including a 2hr catamaran cruise. Choose between morning tea, a buffet lunch, à la carte dinner, or a 1hr 'rocket' between the attractions of the inner harbour.
✉ Darling Harbour's Aquarium Wharf (3, K4) ☎ 9264 7377 ⑤ rocket $18/9; morning tea $24/12; lunch $49.50/24.50; dinner $95/48

STA ferries
If anyone's qualified to show you Sydney Harbour, it's Sydney Ferries. Morning, afternoon and evening 'harbour lights' cruises are available, taking between 1 and 2½ hrs.
☎ 131 500 ❸ www.sta.nsw.gov.au ⑤ $12-17.50

Early morning mist in the Megalong Valley, Blue Mountains National Park

Ross Barnett

Matilda III ready to tour

Bounty
Cruise on the replica *Bounty* made for the film *Mutiny on the Bounty*, starring Mel Gibson. They promise that 'you really do sail' but the boat is often seen ploughing through the harbour waters with all sails down – curious.
✉ **Campbells Cove, The Rocks (3, C7)** ☎ 9247 1789 ⑤ **lunch $55 ($80 weekends), dinner $85, Sunday brunch $45**

Vagabond
Vagabond's 'coffee' cruises ply the inner harbour out to the heads, while 'luncheon' cruises add a swing under the bridge to Darling Harbour. There's devonshire tea and a bar on all boats.
✉ **Circular Quay East (3, E8) & Darling Harbour (3, L3)** ☎ 9660 0388 ⑤ **coffee tours $15-36, lunch $47**

MOTORBIKE TOUR
Blue Thunder
Zip up your leather jacket, clip on your helmet and roar off on the back of a Harley-Davidson. Work out your own itinerary or take a set tour.
☎ 9977 7721 ⑤ **$75/ 125/230 for 1/2/4hrs**

MOVIE STUDIO TOUR
Fox Studios (2, J11)
Fox Studios' 'Backlot Tour' that takes you through The Simpsons lounge room, lets you be an extra on Titanic and hang out with Babe. The 'Lights! Camera! Chaos!' production, with its madcap emu showgirls, has wide appeal.
✉ **Moore Park** ☎ 1300 369 849 🚌 339, 372, 377, 390-9 ⑤ **$37.95/ 22.95 (free for under 6s)** ⏰ **10am-6pm daily**

RAIL TOUR
Long Lunch Train
A restored old train takes passengers south to Moss Vale through bush and farmland before stopping for a gourmet picnic, then travels through Robertson, the spectacular Illawarra coast and Royal National Park.
☎ 1300 653 801 🌐 www.globalpresence. com.au/3801 ⑤ **$90**

SCENIC FLIGHTS
South Pacific Seaplanes
Departing from Rose Bay or Palm Beach, these harbour fly-bys are sure to take your breath away. A 15min flight includes the inner harbour and Harbour Bridge.
☎ 9544 0077 ⑤ **15mins $75/40, 30mins $150/75**

WALKING TOUR
Maureen Fry Walking Tours
The fantastically well-informed Ms Fry offers guided tours of Macquarie St, The Rocks, Paddington and Chinatown – or you can make your own suggestions. Groups and individuals catered for.
☎ 9660 7157 🌐 mpfry @ozemail.com.au ⑤ **$16 for 2hrs (accompanying children free)**

WINE TASTING TOUR
Scenic Wine Tasting Tours
This minicoach tour to the Hunter Valley, 180km north of Sydney and home to more than 70 wineries, includes tastings at 3 wineries and a cheese factory, and lunch at McWilliams Estate.
☎ 9555 2700 🌐 www. redcarpettours.com.au ⑤ **$110/100**

The Bounty docked at Campbells Cove, The Rocks

shopping

Sydney's brash commercialism goes a long way to explaining its citizens' love of shopping. Most see it as recreational activity, rather than necessity. The recent proliferation of weekend markets bears witness to this fact.

Hot Shop Spots

Sydney's main shopping areas are:

City Centre – major department and chain stores, international boutiques, duty free shops, Australiana and outdoor gear

The Rocks – opal stores, Australiana and Aboriginal artefacts

Oxford St, Paddington & Darlinghurst – hip boutiques, bookstores, homewares and speciality stores

Queen St, Woollahra – art galleries and antiques

Double Bay – designer boutiques, expensive childrenswear

King St, Newtown & Crown St, Darlinghurst – quirky clothing, record shops, funky furniture and giftware

Balmain & Glebe – bookstores, vintage clothing, one-off boutiques

Eclectic stores reflect the vibrancy of Newtown's off-beat community.

Shopping in Sydney can be fun, but also hectic. The cramped central business district is full to the brim with department, chain and international fashion stores. Much more relaxed are inner-city shopping strips like Paddington, Glebe and Newtown which offer a variety of boutiques, cafes and cinemas. While you can purchase everything from gumboots to Gucci G-strings, some of the most interesting merchandise in Sydney is found in gallery-stores – Aboriginal artefacts and cutting-edge craft (glass and jewellery), in particular.

All stores accept major credit cards but identification (a valid driver's licence or passport) is required when using travellers cheques. A goods and services tax, or GST, which takes effect in July 2000, will lift the price of most goods by up to 10%.

In general, bargaining is discouraged but it may work at duty free stores and weekend markets. Most of the larger stores are happy to arrange the shipment or mailing of bulky or fragile items.

Opening Hours

Most stores are open from 9am to 5.30pm Monday to Wednesday and Friday, until 9pm Thursday, and 5pm Saturday. Sunday trading is increasingly popular, but expect shorter hours; typically 11am to 4pm. Sales are usually held in early January and July.

Simon Bracken

CLOTHING & JEWELLERY

Collette Dinnigan

Collette Dinnigan's gorgeous shop is the perfect backdrop for her sheer, romantic beaded dresses and flouncy, diaphanous lingerie. With its limewashed floors, wrought iron spiral staircase and courtyard fountain it's easy to pretend you're shopping in a Paris salon.

✉ 33 William St, Paddington (4, H7) ☎ 9360 6691 🚌 378, 380, 382, L82 ⏰ Mon-Wed & Fri-Sat 10am-6pm, Thurs 10am-7pm, Sun 12-4pm

Country Road

For the past 2 decades Country Road has been defining modern Australian fashion. Specialising in contemporary classics in linen, crisp cotton and wool for the office and outdoors, the store also sells stylish homewares.

✉ 142 Pitt St (3, J6) ☎ 9394 1823 🚌 Town Hall; St James ⏰ Mon-Wed 9am-5.30pm, Thurs 9am-9pm, Fri 9am-6pm, Sat 9am-5pm, Sun 11am-5pm

Dinosaur Designs

If Fred and Barney ever decided to open a jewellery store, this is what it would look like. Oversized, jewel-coloured, translucent resin bangles and baubles are interspersed with vibrant sculptural vases and bowls. A smaller selection of sterling silver rings and necklaces pleases funky locals and smart tourists.

Collette Dinnigan shopfront

✉ 399 Oxford St, Paddington (4, J7) ☎ 9361 3776 🚌 378, 380, 382, L82 ⏰ Mon-Sat 10am-6pm, Sun 12-5pm

Dinosaur Designs' creations satisfy function and form.

Mambo Jambo

In 1986, a newly formed league met in an Aussie pub to overthrow the tenets of T-shirt design and, along with them, the canons of Western art. They targeted key elements of (artistic) repute with word-bombs like 'Never mind the Pollocks!' and 'Eyes that follow the viewer around the gallery are no longer deemed clever!' These Dada-ramas formed the ideological platform of what was to become Mambo-rama. More than just big ideas for big T-shirts, these consummate notions would provide the sun 'n' surf servile with art, music, life and credo along with boardshorts, swimwear and sunglasses to wear them with. Many artists have since joined the crusade and made their own waves both here and overseas. Mambo continues to provide for convivial weather, if not the all-clear on convivial taste.

Mambo, it's more than just clothing, it's a culture.

Simon Bracken

Makers Mark

Representing over 100 Australian studio jewellers and designers in a gallery-style store, Makers Mark is renowned for its selection of Argyle diamonds and South Sea pearls. Tasteful hand-blown vases, silk scarves and hand-bound stationery make good presents.

✉ **Shop 4, Chifley Plaza, Chifley Square (3, H7)** ☎ 9231 6800 🚇 **Martin Place** ⏲ **Mon-Wed & Fri 9.30am-6pm, Thurs 9.30am-7pm, Sat 9.30am-4pm**

Australian streetwear and surf labels are also available at **General Pants** (☎ 9299 3565), 391 George St (3, K6) and **Hot Tuna** (☎ 9361 5049), 180 Oxford St, Paddington (4, H5).

Mambo

Ride that fashion wave down Oxford St to Mambo, the cult Australian surf and streetwear store. Colourful, tongue-in-cheek cartoony designs are emblazoned on T-shirts, surfboards, backpacks and bikinis. The store pumps through the day to loud acid jazz music, as Sydney surf grommets persuade their hip parents to purchase everything in sight.

✉ **17 Oxford St, Paddington (4, G4)** ☎ 9331 8034 🚌 **378, 380, 382, L82** ⏲ **Mon-Fri 10am-8pm, Sat-Sun 10am-6pm**

Marcs

Fussy, fashioney men with cash to splurge head to

Makers Mark offers unique jewellery and tasteful gifts.

Marcs for directional Euro and Japanese labels like Diesel Jeans, Dries Van Noten, Yohji Yamamoto and Issey Miyake. Those on a tighter budget make do with Marcs' hip, own-label line of T-shirts, casual pants and suits. Women's and kids' clothes are also available.

✉ Shop P288, Pitt St Mall (3, K6) ☎ 9221 5575 🚇 Town Hall; St James ⏰ Mon-Wed & Fri 9.30am-6pm, Thurs 9.30am-9pm, Sat 9.30am-5.30pm, Sun 10.30am-5pm

Orson & Blake

Known primarily as Sydney's most stylish homewares emporium, Orson & Blake also stocks a great selection of clothes. You'll find up to the minute Australian and New Zealand designers like Vixen, Karen Walker and TL Wood as well as opulent scarves, handbags and jewellery from all corners of the globe.

✉ 83-5 Queen St, Woollahra (4, K9) ☎ 9326 1155 🚌 378, 380, 382, L82 ⏰ Mon-Sat 9.30am-5.30pm, Sun 12-5pm

Paspaley Pearls

Enter this shell-shaped store and admire lustrous South Sea pearls set in classic and modern designs. Prices start at $400 for a ring and rise to more than $650,000 for a strand of the rarer golden pearls. Harvested off the Western Australian coast, the pearls are some of the largest in the world, ranging in colour from silver through to white gold.

✉ 142 King St (3, J7) ☎ 9232 7633 🚇 Martin Place ⏰ Mon-Fri 10am-5.30pm, Sat 10.30am-3.30pm

Saba

Saba is known for its affordably smart suits and knitwear. Overseas trends are translated for male and female urbanites looking for well-cut, long-lasting pieces in their favourite colour – black.

✉ Shop P3, Skygarden, 77 Castlereagh St (3, K6) ☎ 9231 2183 🚇 Town Hall; St James ⏰ Mon-Wed & Fri 9.30am-6pm, Thurs 9.30am-9pm, Sat 9.30am-5pm, Sun 12-5pm

Scanlan & Theodore

Cool jazz plays as willowslim, chic gals stock up on fine knits, fitted suits and sexy but stylish dresses. Fiona Scanlan's designs look toward Europe for quality, tailoring, inspiration and price.

✉ 443 Oxford St, Paddington (4, J7) ☎ 9361 6722 🚌 378, 380, 382, L82 ⏰ Mon-Wed & Fri 10am-6pm, Thurs 10am-8pm, Sat 10am-5.30pm, Sun 12-5pm

All that Glitters

A few more stand-out Sydney jewellers are:

Gemtec – Australian gems in a gallery-like showroom
✉ 51 Pitt St (3, F6) ☎ 9251 1599

Hardy Brothers – establishment jewellery and antiques, not cheap
✉ 77 Castlereagh St (3, K6) ☎ 9232 2422

Victoria Spring – funky but delicate beaded jewellery and homewares for Paddington princesses
✉ 110 Oxford St, Paddington (4, G4) ☎ 9331 7862

Tiffany & Co – grab any trinket, as long as they wrap it in that cute blue box
✉ Chifley Plaza (3, H7) ☎ 9235 1777

Love & Hatred – gothic-looking shop full of contemporary, affordable jewellery by Sydney designers
✉ Strand Arcade (3, J6) ☎ 9233 3441

Anne Schofield – antique jewellery for those with a trust fund
✉ 36 Queen St, Woollahra (4, K8) ☎ 9363 1326

DEPARTMENT STORES & SHOPPING CENTRES

Formidable Chifley Plaza houses international and local designer boutiques.

Simon Bracken

Argyle Stores (3, E6)

The Argyle Stores is a collection of boutiques housed in a collection of 19th-century buildings. It feels like a carriage house that has suddenly become an open-plan mini shopping mall. Of interest are the Australian stores: Dinosaur Designs, Aero Plus, Surf, Dive 'n' Ski and Rivers.

✉ 18-24 Argyle St, The Rocks ☎ 9251 4800 🚌 🚶 🚢 Circular Quay ⏰ Mon-Wed & Fri-Sun 10am-6pm, Thurs 10am-7pm

Chifley Plaza

Don't be put off by the austere formality of this upmarket shopping plaza. The formidable semi-circular façade, high ceilings and inlaid marble floors are meant to make you feel insignificant. Venture past Tiffany, Max Mara and Kenzo to the well chosen Australian stores: Makers Mark (jewellery – p. 60), RM Williams (outback clothes) and Bristol & Brook (slick gifts).

✉ 2 Chifley Square (3, H7) ☎ 9221 4500 🚌 Martin Place ⏰ Mon-Fri 10am-6pm, Sat 10am-5pm

David Jones (3, K7)

What David Jones lacks in contemporary cool it makes up for in traditional style. The ground floor is all marble, mirrored columns, gilded lanterns and massive displays of fresh flowers. Ride the wooden escalators up for designer labels, manchester and a whole floor of children and baby needs. The Market St store

features menswear, top brand electrical goods, homewares and an impressive food hall.
✉ 86-108 Castlereagh St & 66-77 Market St ☎ 9266 5737 🚇 St James ⏲ Mon-Wed & Fri 9.30am-6pm, Thurs 9am-9pm, Sat 9am-6pm, Sun 11am-5pm

Gowings
Four floors of clothes, accessories and camping gear for boys, their dads and even grandpa. Established in 1868, Gowings stocks Australian labels like Drizabone, Bonds, RM Williams and Akubra, plus international brands. The ramshackle 1st floor houses the barber shop, where $8 will buy you a shave and a shear.
✉ cnr George & Market Sts (3, K6) ☎ 9264 6321 🚇 Town Hall 🚌 Sydney Explorer stop 14 ⏲ Mon-Wed & Fri 8.30am-6pm, Thurs 8.30am-9pm, Sat 9am-6pm, Sun 10am-5pm

Grace Bros (3, K6)
Extensive renovations have transformed the once dowdy Grace Bros department store. Now there are 4 Italian cafes, a large electrical department, hip fashion and designer cosmetics.
✉ cnr George & Market Sts ☎ 9238 9111 🚇 Town Hall ⏲ Mon-Wed & Fri-Sat 9am-6pm, Thurs 9am-9pm, Sun 11am-5pm

Queen Victoria Building (3, K5)
Occupying an entire city block, the QVB is Sydney's premier speciality shopping arcade. Tourists visit the 1890s Romanesque-style emporium for its stained glass windows, mosaic tiled floors, wrought iron balconies and grand central dome. Shoppers are equally impressed by more than 200 shops which include Lush cosmetics, General Pants, the ABC Shop and Polo Ralph Lauren.
✉ 455 George St ☎ 9265 6864 🌐 www.qvb.com.au 🚇 Town Hall 🚌 Sydney Explorer stop 14 ⏲ Mon-Wed, Fri-Sat 9am-6pm, Thurs 9am-9pm, Sun 11am-5pm

Skygarden (3, K6)
Skygarden comprises 6 shopping levels with a selection of boutiques and quality chain stores. Grab a snack and an Illy coffee in the atrium food court (6th floor) and browse your way back down to street level through fashion and homewares shops like Saba, Country Road, Ergo and Bed Bath 'n' Table.
✉ 77 Castlereagh St ☎ 9231 1811 🚇 Town Hall; St James ⏲ Mon-Fri 8.30am-6pm, Sat 10am-5pm, Sun 11am-5pm

The Strand Arcade
(3, J6) Elegant, Edwardian and eclectic, The Strand Arcade's stained glass windows, iron lacework balconies and vaulted glass ceiling are the backdrop for 3 floors of boutique shops. Hip Australian designers (Brave, Black Vanity, Ian McMaugh), Australiana stores (Strand Hatters, Opal Treasures) and coffee shops make for a pleasant day's shopping.
✉ 412 George St ☎ 9232 4199 🚇 Town Hall; St James ⏲ Mon-Wed & Fri 9am-5.30pm, Thurs 9am-8pm, Sat 9am-4pm, Sun 11am-4pm

Queen Victoria Building's impressive domed roof

MARKETS

Balmain Market

Balmain market is heaven for lovers of handmade goods. Artisans sell toys, candles, comestibles and jewellery under Moreton Bay fig trees and inside the church hall. Middle Eastern, Asian and vegetarian snacks are also available.

✉ St Andrew's Church, cnr Darling St & Curtis Rd, Balmain (2, F8) ☎ 0418 765736 🚌 441-3 🕐 Sat 8.30am-4pm

Bondi Beach Market

Locals and tourists gather to socialise and shop in between Sunday brunch and sunbaking on the beach. The stock is funky and junky, lots of aromatherapy oils, recycled timber furniture and barely-there dresses mixed with bric-a-brac and vintage clothes.

✉ Bondi Beach Public School, cnr Campbell Pde & Warners Ave, Bondi (2, H14) ☎ 9315 8988 🚉 Bondi Junction then bus 380, 382 or L82 🕐 Sun 10am-4pm

Glebe Market

Inner-city hippies and hipsters make Glebe market their home each Saturday. Once massaged, fed on tempeh burgers and clothed in funky vintage gear, they retire to the adjacent park and chill out to sounds of bongoes and wind chimes.

✉ Glebe Public School, Glebe Point Rd, Glebe (2, H8) ☎ 4237 7499 🚌 431-4 🕐 Sat 9.30am-4.30pm

Paddington Bazaar

Each Saturday over 250 of Sydney's up and coming designers gather at this outdoor market to sell funky fashion, hip homewares, New-Age lotions 'n' potions and sexy silverware. When the buskers, babies and beautiful people get too much, head out to Oxford St for a beer at the Light Brigade Hotel.

✉ 395 Oxford St, Paddington (4, J7)

☎ 9331 2923 🚌 378, 380, 382, L82 🕐 Sat 10am-4pm

Paddy's Market

(3, O4) Unlike most markets in Sydney, Paddy's Market is held indoors and only sells new stuff. With over 1000 stalls there's a hell of a lot of CDs, cheap clothes, shoes, fruit, vegetables and flowers to browse through.

✉ cnr Hay & Thomas Sts, Haymarket ☎ 1300 361 589 🚉 Central 🚌 Sydney Explorer stop 17 🕐 Fri-Sun 9am-4pm

The Rocks Market

Under a 150m-long canopy, stall-holders sell a mix of handmade gifts, antiques, collectibles and craft. Musicians and performers entertain the kids while parents enjoy a pint in the neighbouring Irish pubs.

✉ George St, The Rocks (under Harbour Bridge) (3, D6) ☎ 9255 1717 🚉 🚌 ⚓ Circular Quay 🕐 Sat-Sun 10am-5pm

Sydney Opera House Market

Contemporary, handmade arts and crafts. Worth a visit if you're in the area. Stall-holders include milliners, photographers, painters, ceramicists and jewellers.

✉ Western Boardwalk, Sydney Opera House (3, D8) ☎ 9315 8465 🚉 ⚓ Circular Quay 🚌 438, L38, Sydney Explorer stop 2 🕐 Sun 9am-5pm

Sales beneath the sails at the Opera House Market

Richard I'Anson

ART & ANTIQUES

Gould Galleries
Gould Galleries specialises in investment art. Prominent 20th-century Australian artists are featured on the walls, so expect prices to reflect their importance. Arthur Boyd, Sidney Nolan, Brett Whiteley and Margaret Preston are just a few of the heavy hitters.
✉ 92 Queen St, Woollahra (4, K9) ☎ 9328 9222 ☒ Edgecliff 🚌 378, 380, 382, L82 ⏰ Tue-Sat 11am-6pm, Sun 2-5pm

Sotheby's/Christies
Both of these international auction houses hold sales in Sydney throughout the year. Themes include Aboriginal and tribal art, Colonial furniture, Australian paintings and works on paper. Call for details.
✉ 118 Queen St (4, K10)/180 Jersey Rd (4, J10) Woollahra ☎ 9362 1000/9326 1422 ☒ Edgecliff 🚌 378, 380, 382, L82 ⏰ Mon-Fri 9am-5.30pm/Mon-Fri 9am-5pm

Old-world collectibles

Sydney Antique Centre
Over 60 dealers specialising in Australian and European porcelain, silver, glass, collectibles and furniture display their wares in Sydney's oldest and largest antique centre. The cafe and arts bookshop are an added bonus.
✉ 531 South Dowling St, Surry Hills (4, J3) ☎ 9361 3244 ☒ Central 🚌 339, 340, 373, 374, 390-4 ⏰ 10am-6pm

Woollahra Antique
Similar stock to the Sydney Antique Centre, but the atmosphere's a little dowdy. Fifty dealers are supplemented by an art gallery, cafe, bookshop, gilding and restoration service.
✉ 160 Oxford St, Woollahra (2, J11) ☎ 9327 8840 🚌 378, 380, 382, L82 ⏰ 10am-6pm

ABORIGINAL ART

Aboriginal Art Shop
Tucked neatly into the Opera House's upper concourse is this one-stop Aboriginal art and craft shop. Merchandise includes clapsticks, bull roarers and dillybags as well as more commercial gifts like Tiwi designed sarongs.
✉ Upper Concourse, Sydney Opera House (3, D9) ☎ 9247 4344 ☒🚌⛴ Circular Quay ⏰ 10am-6pm

Aboriginal & Tribal Art Centre
Helpful staff take the time to explain the original use of many of the artefacts displayed in this large shop. Look for pandanas fibre weavings, emu feather baskets and Tiwi designed fabric. The gallery space displays works on paper, canvas and bark by artists from Arnhem Land, Bathurst Island and the Western Desert.
✉ 1st fl, 117 George St, The Rocks (3, E6) ☎ 9247 9625 ☒🚌⛴ Circular Quay ⏰ 10am-5pm

Coo-ee Aboriginal Art
Coo-ee stocks a standard collection of affordable souvenirs, jewellery and artefacts. The upstairs gallery is more interesting with a large range of limited edition prints, sculptures and paintings by urban and desert artists.
✉ 98 Oxford St, Paddington (4, G4) ☎ 9332 1544 🚌 378, 380, 382, L82 ⏰ Mon-Sat 10am-6pm, Sun 11am-5pm

Gavala
Gavala is Sydney's only Aboriginal owned and operated gallery and shop. Aiming to ensure that all products have been purchased directly from the artists, they stock lots of didjeridus, carvings, T-shirts and gifts. The shop is decorated like an outback shed (ochre coloured floors and corrugated iron display walls) with the world's largest boomerang hanging from the roof. Gavala also holds a variety of traditional cultural performances (see page 93).
✉ L2, Harbourside, Darling Harbour (3, L3) ☎ 9212 7232 ☒ Town Hall, monorail, SLR 🚌 888 ⏰ 10am-9pm

OUTDOOR GEAR

Paddy Pallin

Backpackers and outdoor adventure enthusiasts flock to Kent St (between Bathurst and Druitt Sts) where several stores cater to mountaineers, snowboarders, anglers and climbers. Sleeping bags, camping gear and Gortex clothing are among the best sellers. Be sure to compare prices.

✉ 507 Kent St (3, L5) ☎ 9264 2685 🚇 Town Hall, monorail ◷ Mon-Wed 9am-5.30pm, Thurs 9am-9pm, Fri 9am-6pm, Sat 9am-5pm, Sun 10am-4pm

Rebel Sports

This no-frills, one-stop sports store resembles a supermarket. Walk down endless aisles for well priced equipment, clothes, shoes and accessories. Brands include all the faves; Nike, Adidas, Champion and Reebok.

✉ Shop 401, Gallery Level, Mid City Centre, 197 Pitt St (3, K6) ☎ 9221 8633 🚇 Town Hall; St James ◷ Mon-Wed & Fri 9am-6pm, Thurs 9am-9pm, Sat 9am-5pm, Sun 11am-5pm

Surf, Dive 'n' Ski

Up to the minute Australian surf and streetwear labels available in a big, funky, cluttered store. TV monitors blare music videos as good-looking staff sell surf, skate and snowboards to amateurs and pros.

✉ 462 George St (3, L6) ☎ 9267 3408 🚇 Town Hall 🚌 Sydney Explorer stop 14 ◷ Mon-Wed 8.30am-5.30pm, Thurs 8.30am-9pm, Fri 8.30am-6pm, Sat 9am-6pm, Sun 10am-5pm

Woolys Wheels

Two floors of bikes, accessories and related clothing for serious and leisure cyclists alike. Kids love the primary coloured Kettler tricycles, teenagers drool over Mongoose mountain bikes and hipsters opt for electric scooters. A repair shop and bike hire service are also available.

✉ 82 Oxford St, Paddington (4, G4) ☎ 9331 2671 🚌 378, 380, 382, L82 ◷ Mon-Wed & Fri 9am-6pm, Thurs 9am-8pm, Sat 9am-4pm, Sun 11am-4pm

Popular souvenirs: from didjeridus to Ken Done T-shirts

AUSTRALIANA

Australian Conservation Foundation Shop

Want to buy a gift and help save Australian wildlife at the same time? Then follow your ears and nose to the ACF store. Wind chimes, CDs of birdsong and the smell of natural aromatherapy products make this tiny store a heady delight. There's also an eclectic mix of Aboriginal crafts, educational toys and bush-tucker food.

✉ 33 George St, The Rocks (3, D6) ☎ 9247 4754 🚌 🚢 Circular Quay ◷ 10.30am-5.30pm

Australian Wine Centre

A small basement store packed with quality Australian wine, beer and spirits. Pick up a bottle of Yellowglen, smoked salmon and cheese for a picnic or organise a shipment of Wynn's 'Coonawara Estate' back home. Bigger budgets enjoy the small humidor containing Cuban cigars and an impressive range of Penfold 'Grange' wines.

✉ Shop 3, Goldfields House, 1 Alfred St, Circular Quay (3, F6) ☎ 9247 2755 🚇 🚌 🚢 Circular Quay ◷ Mon-Sat 9.30am-6.30pm, Sun 11am-5pm

Done Art & Design

Think Matisse...but on Prozac. Ken Done's optimistic, colourful images of Sydney icons are emblazoned on everything from T-shirts to mousepads. Geared mainly towards the tourist trade, Done is the sunny side of modern Australiana.

✉ 123-5 George St, The Rocks (3, E6) ☎ 9251 6099 🚊 🚌 🚢 Circular Quay ⏰ Mon-Fri 9.30am-7pm, Sat 9.30am-6.30pm, Sun 10am-6pm

Ken Duncan Gallery

Saturated with colour and light, Ken Duncan's panoramic photographs of the Australian landscape induce envy in amateur photographers. Ayers Rock, the Opera House, outback and beach are all captured by his lens. While limited edition prints cost up to $3000, most images can be purchased on more moderately priced posters, jigsaw puzzles and gift-cards.

✉ 73 George St, The Rocks (3, D6) ☎ 9241 3460 🚊 🚌 🚢 Circular Quay ⏰ Mon-Wed &

Fri-Sun 9am-8pm, Thurs 9am-9pm

Opal Fields

Opal Fields stocks a glittering array of Australian opals in their gallery-style store. Starting price is $100 for a pair of triplet earrings, while an opal pendant set in 18 carat gold may set you back thousands.

✉ 155 George St, The Rocks (3, F6) ☎ 9247 6800 🚊 🚌 🚢 Circular Quay ⏰ 9am-9pm

RM Williams

Urban cowboys, country folk and tourists make a bee-line to RM Williams for classic bushman's clothing. The hard-wearing and durable garments look just as good in the city as they do in the outback. Favourites include Akubra hats, Drizabone jackets, moleskin jeans and sturdy leather work boots.

✉ 389 George St (3, K6) ☎ 9262 2228 🚊

Wynyard ⏰ Mon-Wed & Fri 9am-5.30pm, Thurs 9am-9pm, Sat 9am-5pm, Sun 11am-4pm

Wilderness Society Shop

The Wilderness Society campaigns against the destruction of Australian rainforests and waterways. Their retail store assists their efforts. Apart from smelling wonderful (it's the organ oil rubbed into the floorboards), the shop is full of unusual and reasonably priced gifts: wattleseed coffee, delicate marsupial brooches and eucalyptus leaf coasters, to name a few.

✉ Shop C3, Centrepoint, Pitt St (3, K6) ☎ 9233 4674 🚊 Town Hall; St James ⏰ Mon-Wed & Fri 9am-6pm, Thurs 9am-8pm, Sat 9am-5pm, Sun 10am-5pm

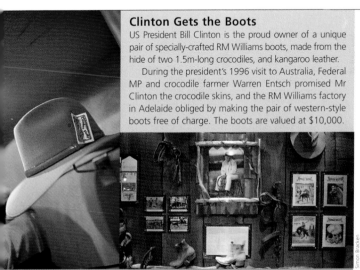

Clinton Gets the Boots

US President Bill Clinton is the proud owner of a unique pair of specially-crafted RM Williams boots, made from the hide of two 1.5m-long crocodiles, and kangaroo leather.

During the president's 1996 visit to Australia, Federal MP and crocodile farmer Warren Entsch promised Mr Clinton the crocodile skins, and the RM Williams factory in Adelaide obliged by making the pair of western-style boots free of charge. The boots are valued at $10,000.

RM Williams' famous bushwear is as popular with city slickers as it is with farmers.

Simon Bracken

MUSIC & BOOKS

ABC Shop

The ABC shop appeals to a broad range of tastes and age groups. Toddlers dash towards the wall of kids' videos, books and sing-along tapes while teenagers covet cult TV T-shirts and comedy videos. Adults are equally pleased by BBC arts videos, classical music recordings and high-brow coffee table books.

✉ Shop 48, L1, QVB, 455 George St (3, K5) ☎ 9333 1635 🚊 Town Hall 🚌 Sydney Explorer stop 14 🕐 Mon-Wed & Fri 9am-5.30pm, Thurs 9am-8pm, Sat 9am-5pm, Sun 11am-5pm

Allans Music

Allans has sheet music and a broad range of instruments for wannabe rock stars, classical musicians and karaoke kings. Brands include Steinway, Roland and Alvarez. DJs hotfoot it to the basement 'groove' room where they can test out drum and mixing machines at ear splitting sound levels.

✉ 333 George St (3, J6) ☎ 9279 4599 🚊 Wynyard 🕐 Mon-Wed & Fri 9am-5.30pm, Thurs 9am-9pm, Sat 9am-5pm

Ariel

Artists, photographers and those in the know congregate throughout the day and late into the night at Ariel. Locals love the wall of glossy design books, hundreds of travel guides and queer lit. section. It's a great place to browse before or after a movie at the Verona or Academy Twin cinemas.

✉ 42 Oxford St,

Paddington (4, G4) ☎ 9332 4581 🚌 378, 380, 382, L82 🕐 9am-midnight

Berkelouw Books

Expecting the smell of musty second-hand books? Forget about it! Follow your nose up the spiral staircase to the cafe for a fix, then browse through pre-loved tomes, antiquarian maps and new releases, spread over 3 floors.

✉ 19 Oxford St, Paddington (4, G4) ☎ 9360 3200 🚌 378, 380, 382, L82 🕐 10am-midnight

Central Station

Club-goers, DJs and dance enthusiasts make their way to this enormous basement store to pick up the latest local and overseas releases. Techno, jungle, hip-hop and house music dominate. Dance party tickets, street-wear and imported magazines are also on offer.

✉ 46 Oxford St, Darlinghurst (4, E1) ☎ 9361 5222 🚊 Central 🚌 378, 380, 382, L82 🕐 Mon-Wed & Fri 10am-7pm, Thurs 10am-9pm, Sat 10am-6pm, Sun 12-6pm

Dymocks

Dymocks' city store stocks 250,000 titles over 3 floors. There are extensive computer, business, stationery and travel sections and staff are young and enthusiastic.

✉ 424-8 George St (3, K6) ☎ 9235 0155 🚊 Town Hall 🕐 Mon-Wed & Fri 9am-6pm, Thurs 9am-9pm, Sat 9am-5pm, Sun 10am-5pm

Folkways

The long-established Folkways stocks jazz, folk and world music CDs. Pressings from Central Asia to the Australian Central Desert are sure to be found here. If not, the staff will order them in.

✉ **282 Oxford St, Paddington (4, H7)** ☎ **9361 3980** 🚌 378, 380, 382, L82 ⊙ **Mon-Wed & Fri-Sat 9am-6pm, Thurs 9am-9pm, Sun 11am-6pm**

Gleebooks

Gleebooks – a ramshackle two-storey terrace house – is widely regarded as Sydney's best bookstore. The aisles are packed with an impressive mix of politics, arts and general fiction and staff know their stuff. Their annual literary program attracts big-name local and international authors. The children's and second-hand book store is at 191 Glebe Point Rd.

✉ **49 Glebe Point Rd, Glebe (2, H8)** ☎ **9660 2333** 🚌 431-4 ⊙ **8am-9pm**

Bargain second-hand reads

HMV

This large British chain store manages to please both the pundits and punters. Comprehensive classical, blues and world music sections are balanced by top 40 CDs, videos and computer games.

✉ **Basement Level, Mid City Centre, Pitt St Mall (3, K6)** ☎ **9221 2311** 🚉 Town Hall; St James ⊙ **Mon-Wed & Fri 8.30am-7pm, Thurs 8.30am-9pm, Sat 9.30am-6pm, Sun 10.30am-5.30pm**

Martin Smith's Bookshop

Do sun-bronzed surfies and tourists read books? If the crowds at Martin Smith's are anything to go by, then the answer must be yes. This tiny cultural hot-spot in the midst of Bondi's literary desert has more books than space, so expect it to feel a bit squirmy. Book-loving staff race up and down wooden ladders to locate over 10,000 titles stocked high to the ceiling.

✉ **3 Hall St, Bondi Beach (2, H13)** ☎ **9365 1482** 🚉 Bondi Junction, then bus 380, 382, L82 ⊙ **9.30am-10pm**

The Bookshop

A large gay and lesbian bookstore in the heart of the Golden Mile. Titles range from queer theory through to erotica and Australian fiction.

✉ **207 Oxford St, Darlinghurst (4, F3)** ☎ **9331 1103** 🚌 378, 380, 382, L82 ⊙ **Mon-Wed 10am-11pm, Thurs-Sat 10am-midnight, Sun 11am-midnight**

FOR CHILDREN

Bow Blue

Painted like the set of a nursery rhyme, Bow Blue is where well behaved little things are bought exquisite outfits, handmade toys and made-to-order dolls' houses. Lines include international labels (Kenzo, Elle, Naf Naf) and less pricey Australian brands (Mambo, Hiawatha, Minoa) for newborns to teens.

✉ **Shops 3 & 4, 74 Castlereagh St (3, K7)** ☎ **9221 6066** 🚉 St James ⊙ **Mon-Wed & Fri 9.30am-6pm, Thurs 9.30am-7pm, Sat 10am-5pm**

Circus Bizircus

Part toy shop, part clothing store, this shop is packed with party frocks, cuddly toys and persuasive kids who know what they want. Parents are smitten as well: mums love the exquisite embroidered bed-linen and dads drool over miniature Formula One Ferraris (a snip at $4450).

✉ **Shop 9, 19-27 Cross St, Double Bay (2, H12)** ☎ **9362 0183** 🚉 Edgecliff, then bus 324, 325, 330 or 365 ⊙ **Mon-Sat 9.30am-6pm, Sun 12-5pm**

David Jones

A cornucopia of expensive wares from formal party dresses to $1000 rocking horses please posh parents, while the rest of us stock up on quality Aussie labels like Fred Bare, Mambo and Gumboots. Kids enjoy the interactive computer displays and parents go gaga over Beatrix Potter and Pooh paraphernalia.

✉ 86-108 Castlereagh St (3, K7) ☎ 9266 5737 🚈 St James ⏲ Mon-Wed & Fri 9.30am-6pm, Thurs 9am-9pm, Sat 9am-6pm, Sun 11am-5pm

Fragile

A chic boutique stocking expensive Euro labels like Petit Bateau, Paul Smith, Diesel, Dries Van Noten and W&LT. Expect to faint at the price tags but drool over handmade soft toys and embroidered bed linen. **The Kids Room** across the road has mid-priced Australian labels like Gumboots and Run, Scotty Run.
✉ 76a Paddington St, Paddington (4, H8) ☎ 9362 0085 🚌 378, 380,

382, L82 ⏲ Mon-Wed & Fri 10am-5.30pm, Thurs 10am-7pm, Sat 10am-5.30pm, Sun 11am-4pm

Kidstuff

Parents seem more excited than their children to discover this small store filled with educational, traditional and low tech toys and games. Aiming to engage and expand kids' minds, Kidstuff mixes well-known brands (Brio, Fisher-Price, Lego) with dress-up costumes, musical instruments and soft toys.
✉ 126a Queen St, Woollahra (4, K10) ☎ 9363 2838 🚈 Edge-cliff, then bus 378, 380, 382 or L82 ⏲ Mon-Fri

9.30am-5.30pm, Sat 9am-4pm

Lesley McKay Children's Bookshop

Smart kids lead their parents to Lesley McKay's, where the shelves are stocked with picture books, pop-ups, jigsaw puzzles and audio tapes. Popular Australian authors (Mem Fox, Alison Lester and John Marsden) are well represented, as are much loved classics by Dahl, Lewis Carrol and AA Milne.
✉ 344 New South Head Rd, Double Bay (2, H12) ☎ 9363 0374 🚈 Edgecliff, then bus 324, 325, 330 or 365 ⏲ Mon-Sat 9am-6pm, Sun 10am-6pm

FOOD & DRINK

Cyril's Delicatessen

Cyril's is a deli in the old style, stocking a fantastic selection (around 4000 different product lines) of mainly European smallgoods, cheeses, biscuits and other delicacies. Cyril Vincent has opened his store at the crack of dawn for 46 years and his loyal customers keep coming back for their jars of Polish pickles and Belgian chocolates at non-gourmet prices.
✉ 183 Hay St, Haymarket (3, O5) ☎ 9211 0994 🚈 Central, monorail, SLR ⏲ Mon-Fri 6am-5.30pm, Sat 6am-1pm

David Jones Food Hall

David Jones' prestigious food hall overwhelms every sense. Noses are led to quality cheeses and coffee, eyes to the seafood and

deli counters while mouths salivate over pastries and chocolate. The hip pocket may baulk at the bill the body runs up.
✉ 66-77 Market St (3, K7) ☎ 9266 5737 🚈 St James ⏲ Mon-Wed & Fri 9.30am-6pm, Thurs 9am-9pm, Sat 9am-6pm, Sun 11am-5pm

Jones The Grocer

High-end groceries, cookbooks and a cafe for lovers of gourmet goodies. There's 2 locations at which to indulge in creamy, Portuguese custard tarts and strong coffee. Similar comestibles and cookware are found near Jones' Woollahra store at **Simon Johnson** (☎ 9328 6888) 55 Queen St, Woollahra (4, K9), and **Fuel** (p. 83) in Surry Hills.
✉ 68 Moncur St, Woollahra (4, K10) & 36

Campbell Pde, Bondi (2, J13) ☎ 9362 1222, 9130 1100 🚈 Edgecliff 🚌 378, 380, 382, L82 ⏲ Mon-Fri 8am-7pm, Sat 9am-5.30pm, Sun 10am-4pm

Kemeny's Liquor Store

Kemeny's proximity to Bondi Beach ensures that many of its customers are clad only in swimming costumes and thongs. The store's casual feel doesn't deter fully-attired wine buffs from snapping up discounted local and imported lines. A small, fine-wine room and extensive beer selection pleases most palates.
✉ 137 Bondi Rd, Bondi (2, J13) ☎ 9389 6422 🚈 Bondi Junction 🚌 380, 382, L82 ⏲ Mon-Sat 8am-9pm, Sun 9am-8pm

La Gerbe d'Or

One of Sydney's most well-loved patisseries, La Gerbe d'Or has been baking mouth-watering sweet and savoury French breads, cakes, pastries and quiches for more than 19 years. The chunky beef burgundy pies are close to legendary, and the croque en bouche a traditional delight.

✉ 255 Glenmore Rd, Five Ways, Paddington (4, G6) ☎ 9331 1070 🚌 378, 380, 382 ⏲ Tues-Fri 8am-7pm, Sat 8am-4pm, Sun 8am-1pm

Macro

The staff at Macro are so herbal and happy that they massage each other in between stocking the shelves. New-Age music plays softly as shoppers purchase rainforest honey, tea-tree soap and organic fruit and vegetables. There's a cafe, juice bar and homeopathic dispensary on site as well.

✉ 31-5 Oxford St, Bondi Junction (2, J12) ☎ 9389 7611 🚉 Bondi Junction 🚌 355, 378, 380, 382, 389, L82 ⏲ Mon-Fri 8am-8pm, Sat 8am-7pm, Sun 9am-6pm

Sweet William Chocolates

This tiny European-style shop sells scrumptious handmade chocolates, including truffles, pralines, nougats, fudges and even soy chocolate, to a discerning clientele. You can buy just one chocolate, or create your own gift box with a selection of your favourites.

✉ 4 William St, Paddington (4, H7) ☎ 9331 5468 🚌 378, 380, 382 ⏲ 10am-6pm

Sydney Fish Market

Chefs, locals and overfed seagulls haggle over still wiggling mud crabs, Balmain bugs and lobsters at Sydney's premier fish market. Located by Blackwattle Bay, this is a busy piscatorial precinct, with retailers, restaurants, seafood school and early morning auctions.

✉ Bank St, Pyrmont (2, G8) ☎ 9660 1611 🚉 Central, then SLR 🚌 443, 501, 888 ⛴ Pyrmont Bay ⏲ 7am-4pm

Ultimo Wine Centre

Sydney's leading import specialist, with wines divided by region and special sections devoted to books and accessories. A regular newsletter alerts customers to upcoming shipments and pre-purchase discounts. The Saturday afternoon wine tastings are especially popular.

✉ 99 Jones St, Ultimo (3, O2) ☎ 9211 2380 🚉 Central, monorail, SLR 🚌 501 ⏲ Mon-Fri 9am-7pm, Sat 10am-8pm, Sun 11am-4pm

Juicy fresh produce

SPECIALIST STORES

Penelope Sach

If Australia has a high priestess of herbal teas, then naturopath Penelope Sach is it. Top restaurants, nervy socialites and the health conscious all rely on her blends to revive and relax. Head to her serene little store to try the best selling Petal and Summer Delight teas.

✉ 2 Moncur St, Woollahra (4, K10) ☎ 9362 3339 🚉 Edgecliff 🚌 378, 380, 382, L82 ⏲ Mon-Fri 9am-5.30pm, Sat 10am-3pm

The Pop Shop

Kitsch, camp and fun, the Pop Shop is an ever-changing mix of completely useless but utterly intriguing gifts and cards aimed at a gay and lesbian clientele.

✉ 143 Oxford St, Darlinghurst (4, F2) ☎ 9331 7849 🚌 378, 380, 382, L82 ⏲ Mon-Wed & Fri-Sat 9am-6pm, Thurs 9am-7.30pm, Sun 10.30am-5.30pm

The Puppet Shop at The Rocks

The Puppet Shop is an underground treasure chest. Hanging from the ceiling, in 4 cave-like rooms, are thousands of marionettes, puppets and toys. Some are antique, some are handmade, some are plastic: all bring out the wonder of childhood.

✉ 77 George St, The Rocks (3, D6) ☎ 9247 9137 🚉 🚌 ⛴ Circular Quay ⏲ 10am-5pm

Simon Bracken

The Strand Hatters

Strand Hatters is to Akubra hats what Bondi Beach is to bare breasts: there are hundreds on display, in all shapes, sizes and colours. The classic Australian bush hat (made from rabbit felt) is stacked high on the shelves among berets, bowlers and panamas. The staff will block and steam hats to customer requirements and for an extra fee provide crocodile teeth hatbands.

✉ Strand Arcade, 412 George St (3, J6) ☎ 9231 6884 🚇 Town Hall; St James ⏰ Mon-Wed & Fri 8am-6pm, Thurs 8am-8pm, Sat 9.30am-4.30pm, Sun 11am-3.30pm

Thirst for Life

Coleridge's Ancient Mariner would be in heaven – water, water everywhere – and it's all bottled and drinkable. This Provençale style boutique is whole-heartedly devoted to H_2O. Sandstone shelves are lined with hundreds of varieties of natural, herbal and fruit flavoured waters from around the world. And before you dismiss the whole idea as a pretentious folly, remember Sydney's 2 water crises in 1998.

✉ 37 William St, Paddington (4, H7) ☎ 9331 6424 🚌 378, 380, 382, L82 ⏰ Mon-Sat 10am-6pm

Elegant Edwardian design at the Strand Arcade

DUTY FREE SHOPS

Allders

Chi-chi mini department store concentrating on exclusive brand cosmetics, alcohol, fragrances and clothes. If Gucci, Cartier, Chanel and Versace make you giddy then you're in the right neighbourhood.

✉ 22 Pitt St (3, F6) ☎ 9241 5844 🚇🚌🚢 Circular Quay ⏰ 10am-10pm

Downtown Duty Free

Sydney's largest duty free chain has recently renovated their flagship city store. Now you can touch and test most of the thousands of items stocked in this always busy shop. In between bargaining for the best price on a new Pentax have a turn on the free Nintendo and Gameboy consoles. DDF also offer a pre-order service (☎ 9319 5599) allowing pick-up of goods at the airport prior to departure.

✉ Basement Level, Strand Arcade, 412-14 George St (3, J6) ☎ 9233 3166 🚇 Town Hall; St James ⏰ Mon-Wed & Fri 9am-5.30pm, Thurs 9am-9pm, Sat 9am-5pm, Sun 11am-4pm

Paxton's Camera & Video

Operating as a retail and tax-free store, Paxton's has a pretty comprehensive selection of new and second-hand cameras, videos and accessories. You can browse through the book section or get some expert advice on the latest digital cameras while your film is being developed.

✉ 285 George St (3, H6) ☎ 9299 2999 🚇 Wynyard ⏰ Mon-Wed & Fri 8.45am-5.30pm, Thurs 9am-8pm, Sat 9-4pm, Sun 10am-3pm

City Savings

The bulk of Sydney's duty-free shops are found in the city centre.

Pitt St is a good place to start, as it has **City International Duty Free** (☎ 9232 1555) at No 88 (3, H6), **Fletchers Fotographics** (☎ 9267 6146) at No 317 (3, L6), **Harbouride Duty Free** (☎ 9281 3666) at No 249 (3, K6) and **Ted's Camera & Video** (☎ 9264 1687) at No 254 (3, L6).

Also worth trying is **Camera House** (☎ 9299 4404) at 416 George St (3, K6).

the olympic games

In September 2000, sports people from all over the globe will converge on Sydney to take part in the world's greatest sporting event – the Olympic Games. For 2 weeks, the eyes of the world will be on these athletes as they aim to achieve their ultimate ambition – to become the first Olympic gold medallists of the new millennium.

ANCIENT OLYMPICS

The Ancient Olympics were held in Olympia, Greece, every 4 years from at least 776 BC. Some evidence dates the Games even earlier, to around 900 BC; other historians believe a similar festival existed at least 4 centuries previously.

Competitors had to be free-born male Greeks. From 750 BC they competed in the nude; prior to that they wore a shorts-like garment. Women and slaves were forbidden, under threat of death, to even attend the Games.

In addition to a crown of wild olive leaves, winners at the ancient Olympics were often richly rewarded by their home states and sometimes became wealthy. The importance of winning at Olympia,

Paralympics

The Paralympics began when the UK government set up a spinal injuries centre for ex-servicemen at London's Stoke Mandeville hospital in 1944. As part of their therapy, patients were introduced to a number of sports, and in 1948 a sports competition involving patients from various rehabilitation centres took place. When Holland joined in 3 years later the international Paralympic movement was born.

and the reflected glory it bestowed on the winner's birthplace, led cities to hire professionals and bribe judges. The farce that the Olympics were to become was symbolised by Nero's appearance in the chariot race in 66 AD: he was drunk, there were no other competitors, and he did not even finish the course, but he was declared the winner.

In 393 AD the Olympics were abolished by the Christian emperor Theodosius, and Olympia was buried under earthquakes until excavated between 1875 and 1881. It was these excavations that led to the resurection of the Games.

Swims like a butterfly: the Olympic swim finals always make a monumental splash.

MODERN OLYMPIC HISTORY

The modern Olympic Games were the brainchild of Frenchman Baron de Coubertin. Inspired by epic tales of the Ancient Olympics and by the public school games of 19th century Britain, he organised a world sports congress in Paris in 1894. The congress spawned the International Olympic Committee and the decision to revive the Olympics in 1896.

De Coubertin intended the Games to be for amateurs only (with the exception of professional fencing masters); that competitors should be adult males; and that the Olympics should be held every 4 years in different venues. The only stipulation that has stood the test of time is that the Games are held in different cities.

The 1896 Games, funded by a wealthy Greek architect, a lottery, and the world's first collection of sporting postage stamps, were well attended and successful. However, the following two Games, held in Paris and St Louis, were appalling: they were staged as an appendage to the World Exhibition, and the sporting events were held over a period of several months. Additionally, the organisation was so bad that in Paris many competitors had no idea they were taking part in the Olympics, and in St Louis many of the events were open only to Missouri residents.

The Fairer Sex

When women made their Olympic debut, in Paris in 1900, they were only permitted to compete in 'genteel' sports like tennis and golf. Women's swimming and highboard diving were added to the program in 1912, but track and field events did not make it until 1928. Unfortunately, so many competitors collapsed after the 800m race that the distance was declared unsafe for women; it wasn't until 1960 that women were again permitted to run further than 200m in Olympic Games.

The success of the Olympics ebbed and flowed over the next 2 decades. WWI prevented the 1916 Games from taking place, but the 1920 Games, held in war-torn Antwerp, went ahead – a major achievement for the Olympic movement.

The post-WWI years saw increased public interest in the Games, with distance runner Paavo Nurmi and swimmer Johnny Weissmuller (who later played Tarzan in the films of the 1930s and 40s) becoming the first 'household names' of Olympic sport. The 1920s and 30s also witnessed the gradual admission of more female competitors, with women's track and field and gymnastics included in Amsterdam in 1928. The final Games before the outbreak of WWII were held in Berlin, where the Nazi propaganda machine used them to present the image of a democratic, peace-loving Third Reich. This use of the Olympics as a political tool was just a taste of what was to come.

The Soviet invasion of Hungary, Czechoslovakia and Afghanistan, the apartheid regimes of South Africa and Rhodesia, and the British intervention in the Suez crisis resulted in boycotts being a feature of Olympic Games held between 1954 and the end of the Cold War era. The boycotts hit their peak in 1980 when the USA, Canada and Germany refused to attend the Moscow Olympics because of the Soviet invasion of Afghanistan. Four years later the Soviets and most of their East European satellites replied by boycotting the Los Angeles Olympics.

The tragic murder of 11 Israeli athletes by Palestinian terrorists during the 1972 Munich Games led to repeated calls for the Games to end. Countries were becoming loathe to stage an event that had become a security and financial nightmare.

But the success of the 1984 LA Games changed all that. Using marketing, sponsorship and revenue from television rights, LA turned the Games into a huge money spinner. Four years later professional sportspeople were admitted to the Olympics, and in 1989/90 the Eastern bloc dismantled, ending tit-for-tat boycotts.

In 1998-9 the IOC was forced to admit that some of its officials had accepted bribes from the organising committee of the Salt Lake City Games of 2002. In 1999 Australian Olympic Committee president John Coates admitted that inducement payments were made to Kenyan and Ugandan officials to encourage them to vote for the Sydney bid.

The anger these revelations provoked among athletes, sports fans and the organisers of failed Olympic bids resulted in IOC President Juan Antonio Samaranch ordering an inquiry into the bribery scandal. But news that he had received gifts from 2 bid cities shortly before these cities won rights to hold the Games did not instil critics with confidence in his ability to weed out corruption.

At present corruption and drugs – and the IOC's perceived soft line on both – pose the greatest threat to the future of the Greatest Show on Earth. But whatever else happens in Sydney, it will be the performances of the next Carl Lewis or Nadia Comaneci that will be remembered after other events have been forgotten.

The Olympic Torch

The world has the Nazis to thank for the concept of the Olympic flame and torch relay. The brainchild of Carl Diem, head of the organising committee for the Berlin Olympics, the Olympic flame was ignited in Olympia, Greece, for the first time in 1936, and was carried from there to Berlin by 3075 torchbearers, all running just slightly over 1 mile of the journey.

The Sydney 2000 Olympic Torch Relay will travel over 27,000km and be carried by 10,000 torchbearers in what is the longest torch relay in Olympic history.

Apart from being carried by torchbearers, the Olympic flame will travel on a surf boat at Bondi Beach, on the *Indian Pacific* train across the Nullarbor Plain, on a Royal Flying Doctor Service aircraft in the remote outback, and by camel on Cable Beach at Broome. Before reaching Australia, the torch will be taken by plane to Guam, where it will begin a 20-day journey visiting the 12 Pacific Island countries that make up the Oceania ring of the Olympic nations. It will then visit every state and territory in Australia over 100 days. The first person to carry the torch in Australia will be Australian Olympic hockey gold medallist-turned-sprinter Nova Peris-Kneebone.

THE SYDNEY GAMES

The 2000 Olympic Games will take place in Sydney from 15 September to 1 October, bringing together more than 10,000 people from 198 countries.

The Sydney games will feature 28 sports (7 of which include multiple disciplines – eg, swimming, diving, synchronised swimming and water polo are all disciplines in the sport of aquatics).

Shortly after the Olympic Games have finished, disabled sportspeople from some 125 countries will converge on Sydney for the 2000 Paralympic Games, held from 18 to 29 October.

For up-to-the-minute information on all the events, check the daily papers and the official Games web site (www.Sydney.Olympic.org), or call the information line on ☎ 13 63 63.

Venues

Most of the Olympic events will take place at Sydney Olympic Park in Homebush Bay, with some sports being held in Sydney West, Sydney East and Darling Harbour.

The centrepiece of Sydney Olympic Park is the 110,000-capacity Stadium Australia. The stadium will stage the opening and closing ceremonies as well as the athletics events and the football (soccer) final.

Also in Olympic Park is the Sydney International Aquatic Centre, which holds 17,500 people. The gymnastics events and the basketball finals will be held in the 18,000-seater Sydney Superdome. The Baseball Stadium (main arena), Hockey Centre, Tennis Centre and Bicentennial Park (where the modern pentathlon will take place) are also in Olympic Park.

Sydney West will stage the water polo at Ryde Water Polo Pool, rowing and canoeing at the Regatta Centre in Penrith, the cycling at Dunc Gray Velodrome, Bankstown, and the 3-day eventing at the appropriately named Horsley Park.

In Sydney East, there's sailing at Rushcutters Bay, beach volleyball at Bondi Beach, and football at Sydney Football Stadium.

Boxing, weightlifting, judo and fencing will be held at the Sydney Exhibition Centre and Convention Centre in Darling Harbour. Preliminary football matches will take place at various venues in Australia: the Gabba in Brisbane, the Hindmarsh Stadium in Adelaide, Canberra's Bruce Stadium and Melbourne's MCG.

Most Medals

Because of the large number of inter-linked gymnastics events (8 for men, 6 for women), Olympic medal-winning records tend to be held by gymnasts. Larissa Latynina (USSR) won a record 18 medals from 1956 to 1964, comprising 9 gold, 5 silvers and 4 bronzes. The record for the most individual golds is 7 by Vera Caslavska (Czechoslovakia) in 1964 and 1968. Nikolai Andrianov (USSR) holds the record for the most Olympic medals by any male competitor in any sport, with a total of 15.

Stadium Australia, Homebush Bay

Chris Elfes / Sport • The Library •

Tickets

Olympic tickets cost A\$105-1382 for the opening and closing ceremonies, A\$65-455 for athletics, and A\$30-80 for rowing. Tickets for blue ribbon events were sold out by September 1999. However, tickets for some sports will possibly remain on sale right up to and during the Games. As at all Olympic Games, scalpers will be out in force, but it's likely that for the less popular events tickets will be available at the door on the day. Keep an eye on the official Olympic web site (www.sydney.olympic.org) or call ☎ 13 63 63 to find out which events can still be attended. Paralympics and arts festival tickets went on sale in October 1999.

Overseas visitors can purchase tickets for the Olympics through agents appointed by their National Olympic Committee. See the NOC's web site (www.olympic.org/family/noc/noc_list.html) for a list of all the Committees around the world where you can purchase a ticket. Some National Olympic Committees are listed below.

A weight-watcher's delight, Atlanta 96

David Callow / Sport • The Library

Australia
(☎ 61-2-9245 2000; fax 9245 2098)
L13, The Maritime Centre, Kent St 207, Sydney NSW 2000

France
(☎ 33-1-40782800; fax 40782951)
Maison du Sport Français,
1 avenue Pierre de Coubertin,
F-75640 Paris Cedex 13

Germany
(☎ 49-69-6700202; fax 6771229)
Postfach 71 02 63,
D-60492 Frankfurt-am-Main

Japan
(☎ 81-3-34812286; fax 34810977)
1-1-1 Jinnan, Tokyo 150-8050

New Zealand
(☎ 64-4-385 0070; fax 385 0090)
Olympic House, 3rd fl, Courtenay Place 97-9, Wellington

UK
(☎ 44-208-871 2677; fax 871 9104)
Wandsworth Plain 1, London SW18 1EH

USA
(☎ 1-719-632 5551; fax 632 4180)
Olympic House, 1750 East Boulder St, Colorado Springs, CO 80909-5764

The Marathon

Named after the plain outside Athens, site of the Athenians' battle against vastly superior Persian forces in 490BC, the marathon of the modern Olympics honours the messenger Pheidippides' epic run of more than 500kms to enlist the help of the Spartans. Unsuccessful in his mission, the Athenians were nevertheless victorious and later historians recorded that after running the 26 mile and 385 yard (about 42km) distance from Marathon to Athens to deliver the news of the unexpected victory, he collapsed and died of exhaustion.

Although today's marathon is no match for Pheidippides' feat of endurance, the re-enactment of the last leg of his run is considered the pinnacle of the Games and takes place immediately prior to the closing ceremony. At a time when getting a ticket to an Olympic event can be wildly expensive, the marathon remains a people's event and will be run through the streets of Sydney to a cheering crowd.

Freebies

You don't have to be wealthy to watch Olympic sport live. In fact, some of the Sydney events can be seen free of charge. These are:

Marathons The women's marathon will take place from 9am on 24 September, and the men's will be on 1 October from 4pm (followed by the closing ceremony). The 42km course runs from North Sydney Oval through the city centre and out to Stadium Australia in Homebush. Thousands are expected to watch from the roadside.

Dead Good
In the Ancient Olympics, the pankration event was a brutal combination of boxing and wrestling in which virtually anything was permitted. Arrachion of Phigalia was awarded the title in 564 BC because his opponent 'gave up' – though Arrachion himself was by then lying dead in the arena. He remains the only dead person to become an Olympic champion.

Remarkable Performer
In 1904 American gymnast George Eyser won 3 gymnastics events, despite the fact that he was well over 30 and had a wooden leg! Incredibly, he also competed in the all-around track and field contest (forerunner of the decathlon).

Racewalking The men's 20km and 50km walks and the women's 20km walk will also take place on Sydney's streets, on 22, 28 and 29 September.

Cycling The road race route will go through Sydney's eastern suburbs, starting and finishing at Moore Park. Road racing can be seen on 25 (training only), 26 and 27 September.

Triathlon Spectators will be able to watch the swimming stage of this event free from the harbour-side. The event will take place from 10am-1pm on 16 and 17 September.

Sailing Sydney's famous harbour will play host to the sailing events. Yachts will carry special symbols, probably their national flag, to help spectators identify them. The sailing events will take place daily from 16 to 30 September, starting at noon.

In addition to the sporting events, free concerts and street entertainment will be provided for the duration of the Games. These events will be centred on Olympic Boulevard and Millennium Parklands at Homebush Bay, and around the waterfront at Circular Quay and Darling Harbour.

Feats of strength and endurance: canoeing, team pursuit cycling and gymnastics.

Transport

Games ticket holders can travel free on the Sydney Olympic transport system on the day of the event until 4am the following day. Transport will run 24hrs a day. The system covers all CityRail trains and the bus network servicing the venues.

Olympic Park train station will run up to 30 trains an hour and there will be frequent buses to Olympic Park and the other venues. The free transport zone includes central Sydney and extends to Newcastle, Dungog and Scone in the north of NSW, to Port Kembla and Nowra in the south, Coulbourn in the south-west and Bathurst in the west.

Chris Elfes / Sport • The Library

Sydney's state-of-the-art aquatic centre

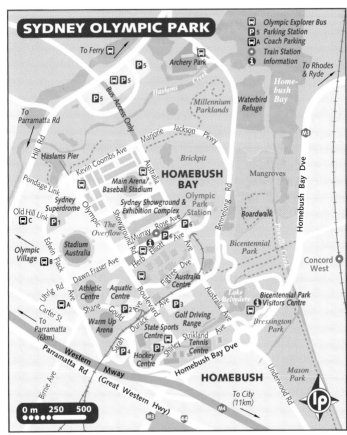

Accommodation

Finding accommodation during the Olympics will be tough; it's best to book as far ahead as possible. Prices for all types of accommodation are expected to skyrocket, and bookings will need to be made in blocks, for a minimum of 3 nights or even 3 weeks for some places.

Sydney only has a limited number of hotel rooms, and many of these will be taken by official and corporate visitors on pre-booked ticket and accommodation packages. So you may need to explore other options.

A diverse range of accommodation is available, from top-end hotels and furnished apartments, to caravans, hostels and B&B-style home-stays. Accommodation is available near the main Olympic venues, in the inner-city suburbs, the outer suburbs and way out of town, as far as Katoomba.

Restaurants

Getting a table at a harbourside restaurant during the Games is likely to be about as easy as getting a hotel room in The Rocks; the truth is, it may be close to impossible. Many of the better Sydney eateries have entered sponsorship deals with the corporate set and will be booked out for the duration of the Games.

The solution? Head to the suburbs, away from the harbour and the main sports venues, or hit the supermarket for a spot of self-catering. Suburban 'eat streets', many of which are literally lined with restaurants, will probably be busier than usual, but at least their doors will be open. The following restaurant strips have a mixed bunch of eateries, serving Modern Australian cuisine unless otherwise noted:

Blues Point Rd, McMahons Point (2, F9)

Broughton St, Kirribilli (2, F10)

Campbell Pde, Bondi (2, H14)

Cleveland St (Lebanese) (2, J10) &
    Crown St (4, G1), Surry Hills

Coogee Bay Rd & Arden St,
    Coogee (2, K12)

Darling St, Balmain (2, F8)

Enmore Rd, Enmore (2, J7)

Glebe Point Rd, Glebe (2, H8)

King St, Newtown (2, J8)

Liverpool St (Spanish), Sydney (3, N8)

Marrickville Rd (Vietnamese),
    Marrickville (2, K6)

Ramsay St (Italian), Haberfield (2, H5)

Stanley St (Italian), East Sydney (4, D1)

The Corso, Manly (2, B14)

Willoughby Rd, Crows Nest (2, D9)

Shopping centre foodcourts also offer a wide selection of cuisines, though it won't always be top notch.

If you've got your heart set on eating at one of Sydney's finer establishments, it may still be worth trying to book a table; some of the city's top restaurateurs have shunned corporate bookings and have vowed to keep their doors open to the public.

places to eat

Other Australian states hate to admit it, but in the food stakes, Sydney has won the trifecta. Its multicultural melange, abundant fresh produce and geographic assets have made it a great city in which to dine. Adelaide may have fine local wines, Melbourne a vibrant cafe culture, but Sydney has both, plus the magnificent harbour.

Newtown, Bondi and Darlinghurst buzz with trendy cafes, Leichhardt is full of Italian bistros and the Haymarket precinct is home to hundreds of Chinese restaurants. As the gentrification of inner-city suburbs spreads, more and more corner pubs are transforming into modern brasseries, local laundromats are installing espresso machines and locals are finding their own kitchens increasingly superfluous.

Sydney Cuisine

A national cuisine, often referred to as Modern Australian (or Mod Oz), continues to evolve, as chefs look to Asia for ingredients and Europe for technique. Cooking focuses on fresh produce and healthy eating while drawing on the rich influences from the migrant community.

Meal Costs
The price ranges in this chapter indicate the cost of a 3-course meal for 1 person (excluding alcohol).

$	$15 and under
$$	$16-25
$$$	$26-50
$$$$	over $50

At the top end of the scale, celebrity chefs plate up mini-masterpieces for a wealthy and corporate crowd. Those on tighter budgets need not despair; thousands of cafes, bistros and restaurants offer innovative, quality meals at moderate prices.

Liquor

Licensing laws in Sydney are gradually being modernised. For the moment, however, many licensed restaurants cannot serve patrons alcohol unless they order a meal. Most restaurants have notable wine lists, emphasising local and interstate product. Prices range from $15-50 a bottle; the average being about $25. There is growing trend to offer a variety of wines by the glass rather than just the house wines. You can also bring your own alcohol to restaurants which advertise that they're 'BYO' – see page 79 for details.

Opening Hours

Cafes and restaurants are generally open 7 days, with many of the former serving food from 8am through to 10pm. Most restaurants are open for lunch and dinner, while cafes and patisseries are the best for breakfast.

BALMORAL

Awaba $$
Mod Oz
Awaba's stark all-white interior is a perfect visual sorbet for the astounding table-side views of Balmoral beach. Surfies and socialites sit side-by-side munching on wood-fired toast with scrambled eggs. Prepare to queue on weekends.
✉ **67 The Esplanade (2, D12)** ☎ **9969 2104** 🚉 **Taronga Park Zoo, then bus 238** ⏱ **7.30am-3pm daily, dinner Wed-Sat 6-10pm** ♿ **yes**

Beach views are a drawcard at Awaba.

Bondi Eats
While in Bondi, also try the ultra-chic **Dig** (☎ 9365 6044), at 56 Campbell Pde (2, H14), for its Mod Oz seafood fare. **Sports Bard** (☎ 9130 4582), at 32 Campbell Pde, is not your average sports cafe. Yes, the walls are crammed with paraphernalia, but the eclectic meals – from schnitzel to spring rolls – have flair and gusto.

BONDI & NORTH BONDI

To get to Bondi beach and North Bondi, take a train to Bondi Junction, then catch bus 380, 382 or L82.

Gusto $
Cafe
Gusto is where Bondi's beautiful people meet, in between sessions with their personal trainers. The food, a quality selection of deli items and salads, is pricey but worth it. Sit outside on milk crates or bar stools and enjoy the passing parade.
✉ **16 Hall St, Bondi (2, H13)** ☎ **9130 4565** ⏱ **6.30am-7pm** ♿ **yes**

Indochine $$
Vietnamese
Modestly priced Vietnamese food in modest surrounds. The fare is consistently good and interesting, from Atlantic salmon in banana leaf to grilled prawns on sugar cane. Book ahead for weekends.
✉ **99 Bondi Rd, Bondi (2, J13)** ☎ **9387 4081** ⏱ **5.30pm-10pm** ♿ **yes**

Jackies $$$
Mod Oz
Jackies' transformation from hip cafe to sleek modern restaurant is complete. The almost all-white interior offers views of Bondi beach while you sup on the light Mediterranean-Oz fare. Big weekend breakfasts always draw a crowd.
✉ **132 Warners Ave, North Bondi (2, H14)** ☎ **9300 9812** ⏱ **Mon-Fri 6pm-midnight, Sat-Sun 9am-midnight** ♿ **yes**

Jed's Foodstore $
Mod Oz Cafe
It seems that all of Bondi heads to Jed's for breakfast. Originally a butcher's shop, it now resembles a funky farmhouse kitchen. The groovy clientele starts the day with Baby Jay's Seratonin juice and Bircher muesli with toasted pistachios and rhubarb.
✉ **cnr Glenayr & Warners Avenues, North Bondi (2, H13)** ☎ **9365 0022** ⏱ **Mon-Fri 7am-6.30pm, Sat-Sun 8am-5.30pm** ♿ **yes**

Raw Bar $$
Japanese
Bondi's movers and groovers share big plates of sushi, sashimi and tempura at this bento-box sized restaurant. Views of Bondi beach are a bonus.
✉ **cnr Warners & Wairoa Aves, North Bondi (2, H14)** ☎ **9365 7200** ⏱ **12-10pm** ♿ **yes**

Speedos $
Cafe
Speedos panoramic view of Bondi beach goes a long way to explain its popularity. Over-taxed waitresses and hit-and-miss dishes are readily forgiven by patrons, who are hypnotised by the scenery. The inexpensive, weekday special of eggs with everything is favoured by surfies and tourists alike. Bookings necessary on weekends.
✉ **126 Ramsgate Ave, North Bondi (2, H14)** ☎ **9365 3622** ⏱ **6.30am-7pm** ♿ **yes**

BRONTE

Sejuiced   S
Cafe
Bondi's little sister, Bronte beach has a thriving food scene. Sejuiced, a small beachside cafe in a row of lookalikes, does stand-out breakfasts and juices. All manner of egg dishes are supplemented by organic banana bread or couscous with dried fruit.
✉ 487 Bronte Rd (2, J13) ☎ 9389 9538 🚇 Bondi Junction, then bus 378 ⏱ 6.30am-7pm ♿ yes

Start the day with a caffeine kick and hearty feed at Jed's Foodstore, North Bondi.

CHINATOWN

For excellent Cantonese-style cuisine and yum cha, head to Chinatown. To get there catch a train to Central, take the monorail or SLR to Haymarket, or catch a ferry to Darling Harbour and stroll south a short way.

BBQ King   S
Cantonese
Low on ambience, but big on flavour, BBQ King serves up ample portions of roast duck, suckling pig and other Cantonese staples. Its late opening hours make it a popular post-cinema haunt.
✉ 18-20 Goulburn St, (3, N5) ☎ 9267 2433 ⏱ 11.30am-2am ♿ yes

Duck in for a Chinatown speciality

Bodhi Vegetarian Restaurant   S
Vegan/Asian
Bodhi's daily dim sum dumplings and dinnertime beancurd claypots attract a funky, young crowd. Bookings advisable.
✉ 730 George St (3, O5) ☎ 9212 2828 ⏱ lunch 10am-3pm, dinner 5-10pm ♿ yes V

Golden Century $$$
Cantonese
Renowned for their seafood, this bustling restaurant offers crustaceans straight from the tank. Abalone, king crab, coral trout and barramundi are cooked to order. Those with money to splash go for whole lobster cooked in ginger and shallots. Bookings advisable.
✉ 393 Sussex St, (3, N5) ☎ 9281 1598 ⏱ noon-4am ♿ yes

Kam Fook   S
Chinese
Queue up with the rest of Sydney for Kam Fook's legendary Sunday yum cha. Amid the constant clatter of more than 800 other diners, an infinite variety of dim sum, congee, rice rolls and custard tarts are trolleyed past the table. The only challenge is to know when to stop eating.
✉ L3, 9 Hay St, Haymarket (3, O5) ☎ 9211 8988 ⏱ lunch Mon-Sat 10am-4pm, dinner Mon-Sun 5.30-11pm, yum cha Sun 9am-4.30pm ♿ yes

Sussex Centre   S
Food Court
Newly renovated, this slick food court offers quick Vietnamese, Malaysian, Korean, Chinese and Japanese meals. Illuminated photos of hundreds of dishes face hungry diners; all you have to do is point and pay. Particularly good is the seafood laksa from *Happy Chef*.
✉ 401 Sussex St, Sydney (3, N5) ☎ 9281 5832 ⏱ 9am-9.30pm ♿ yes

CITY CENTRE

Ampersand $$$$
French/Japanese
Tony Bilson's newest venture overlooks the waterfront at Cockle Bay. Sophisticated, stylish decor is matched by equally smart dishes, such as tartare of whiting with sea urchin roe. Bookings advisable.
✉ **Roof Terrace, L2, Cockle Bay wharf, Darling Park (3, K4)** ☎ **9264 6666** 🚉 **Town Hall, monorail, SLR** 🚌 **888** 🚢 **Darling Harbour** ⏲ **lunch Mon-Fri 12-3pm, dinner Mon-Sat 7-10.30pm** ♿ **no**

Bambini Espresso $
Cafe
Legal eagles and snappy suits crowd into this mini, modern cafe each lunchtime. The lure? Speedy service, gourmet baguettes and vivifying coffees.
✉ **299 Elizabeth St (entrance on Liverpool St) (3, N6)** ☎ **9261 3331** 🚉 **Museum, monorail** ⏲ **Mon-Fri 7am-5.30pm** ♿ **no**

Simon Bracken

Chinta Ria's dramatic Buddhist centrepiece

Banc $$$$
French
Banc's impeccably stylish French menu and luxurious fit-out make it the ideal location for business lunches and important dinners. Negotiate your way through the 20 page wine list, then order à la carte or from the degustation menu. Bookings advisable.
✉ **53 Martin Pl (3, J7)** ☎ **9233 5300** 🚉 **Martin Place** 🚢 **Circular Quay** ⏲ **lunch Mon-Fri 12-2.30pm, dinner Mon-Sat 6.30-10.30pm** ♿ **yes**

The Cafe $
Afternoon Tea
Go on, you deserve it, a little bit of luxury, at a diminutive price. Sixteen dollars buys a full afternoon tea (sandwiches, cakes and hot drinks) at the Regent Hotel's genteel cafe. Courteous staff add to the pleasure.
✉ **199 George St (3, F6)** ☎ **9255 0230** 🚉 🚌 🚢 **Circular Quay** ⏲ **6.30am-11.30pm** ♿ **yes**

Chinta Ria $$
Malaysian
Malaysian hawker-style food served in a dramatic Asian temple/market setting. Go with a gang of friends and share plates of Hokkien noodles, sambal prawns and flaky roti bread.
✉ **Roof Tce, L2, Cockle Bay wharf, Darling Park (3, K4)** ☎ **9264 3211** 🚉 **Town Hall, monorail, SLR** 🚌 **888** 🚢 **Darling Harbour** ⏲ **lunch Mon-2.30pm, dinner 6-10.30pm** ♿ **yes** Ⓥ

Edna's Table $$$$
Australian/Bush
Edna's Table is Sydney's leading exponent of 'bush tucker' (bush food). A successful combination of native ingredients and European technique creates dishes like gumleaf smoked grilled salmon and kangaroo prosciutto salad. The wattleseed pavlova is a winner. Bookings advisable.
✉ **204 Clarence St (3, L5)** ☎ **9267 3933** 🚉 **Town Hall; Wynyard** ⏲ **lunch Mon-Fri 12-3pm, dinner Tues-Sat 6-10pm** ♿ **yes**

> ### Working Lunch
> If you're in town on business, **Ampersand** (this page), **Odeon** (p. 82) and **Banc** (this page) provide a private, comfortable atmosphere where you can meet your clients.

Kingsleys Australian Steakhouse $$$
Australian/Bush
Carnivorous appetites will be sated after a visit to Kingsleys, where aged rib eye, kangaroo fillet and chargrilled lamb are just a few of the menu's meaty items.
✉ **29a King St (3, J5)** ☎ **9262 4155** 🚉 🚌 **Wynyard** ⏲ **lunch Mon-Fri 12-3pm, dinner Mon-Sat 6-10pm** ♿ **yes**

MCA Cafe $$$
Seafood
Vie for a table on the balcony overlooking the Opera House, order the beer-battered fish with yams and tzatziki and praise Sydney's abundant gifts of topography and top

chefs. Try to book ahead for a table.

✉ 140 George St, The Rocks (3, E6) ☎ 9241 4253 🚇 🚌 🚢 Circular Quay ⏱ Mon-Fri 11am-4pm, Sat-Sun 9am-3.30pm 👶 no

MLC Centre $
Food Court
There's a good range of quality city food courts in Sydney – MLC is one of the most popular, with outdoor seating and Italian, Chinese, Mexican and Japanese just some of the cuisines on offer.

✉ 19-29 Martin Pl (3, J7) ☎ 9224 8333 🚇 Martin Place ⏱ Mon-Fri 9am-6pm, Sat 9am-3pm

Mother Chu's Vegetarian Kitchen $
Asian/Vegan
Mother Chu's vegan victuals blend Chinese, Taiwanese and Japanese ingredients. Creations like sizzling stuffed beancurd and claypot chilli noodles are popular and inexpensive.

✉ 367 Pitt St (3, N6) ☎ 9283 2828 🚇 Town Hall, monorail, SLR ⏱ lunch Mon-Fri 12-3pm, dinner daily 5-10pm 👶 yes **V**

Restaurant CBD $$$
Brasserie
Weave your way through the slick, city stockbrokers at the bar to the restaurant upstairs. There you'll find sturdy, boys-own meals like beef sausages and roasted hare, as well as well crafted desserts. Bookings advisable.

✉ L1, 75 York St (3, J5) ☎ 9299 8911 🚇 🚌 Wynyard ⏱ Mon-Fri

lunch 12-3pm, dinner 6-10pm 👶 no

The Sydney Cove Oyster Bar $$$
Seafood
Views of the Harbour Bridge and a plate of freshly shucked rock oysters make for an idyllic Sydney lunch. The setting, a breezy, heritage cottage by the Opera House, almost compensates for the standard seafood fare.

✉ 1 Circular Quay East (3, E8) ☎ 9247 2937 🚇 🚌 🚢 Circular Quay ⏱ Mon-Sat 11am-midnight, Sun 11am-9pm 👶 no

Wockpool $$$-$$$$
Mod Oz
Neil Perry recently moved the much-loved Wockpool to Darling Harbour. Panoramic views and pricey pan-Asian cuisine are the draw. Be sure to try the spanner crab and

green pawpaw salad. Book to be sure.

✉ IMAX Theatre, Cockle Bay, Darling Harbour (3, L4) ☎ 9211 9888 🚇 Town Hall, monorail, SLR 🚌 888 🚢 Darling Harbour ⏱ lunch 12-3pm, dinner 6-10pm

CLOVELLY

Direction of Cure $
Food for the soul and the sweet tooth. Homeopathic remedies and medicinal teas sit alongside indulgent cakes, salads and sandwiches. Their handy picnic packs are great to enjoy on nearby Clovelly beach.

✉ 23a Burnie St (2, K13) ☎ 9665 5244 🚌 339, X39 (from Wynyard station) or 329 (from Bondi Junction) ⏱ Tues-Sun 7am-4pm 👶 yes **V**

A visual feast awaits at Sydney Cove Oyster Bar.

Richard I'Anson

Tipping
While tipping is not yet an entrenched practice, a 10% tip is customary for good service. However, feel free to vary the amount depending on your level of satisfaction. If you're paying by credit card, leave the tip in the tip jar usually provided rather than adding it to the cost of the bill.

DARLINGHURST

To get to Victoria St, Liverpool St and Darlinghurst Rd, take a train to Kings Cross, or bus 330, 323-7, 365, 366, 387 or L24. For Oxford and Crown Sts, catch bus 378, 380, 382 or L82.

Balkan Continental Restaurant $$$
Continental European
Need a hearty feed? Then Balkan is the answer. Recently renovated, the restaurant serves its classic grill menu to ravenous inner-city ragers. Big serves of grilled calamari, schnitzel and fillet mignon hit the spot. Bookings advisable.
✉ **209 Oxford St (4, F2)** ☎ **9360 4970**
🕐 **Mon, Wed, Thurs & Sun 11am-11pm, Fri-Sat 11am-midnight** ♿ **yes; ½ serves available**

bills' mineral water

Bar Coluzzi $
Italian Cafe
Opened in 1957, this unprepossessing little Italian cafe introduced Sydney to espresso coffee. Food is basic, mainly filled focaccias and croissants, but the scene is heady. Sit streetside and network with the mobile phone wielding media folk.
✉ **322 Victoria St (4, D4)** ☎ **9380 5420**
🕐 **5am-7.30pm ♿ yes; ½ serves available**

bills $$
Mod Oz
Sydney loves bills, and for good reason – the sparse, light-filled room belies the wonders created in the kitchen. Breakfast staples include ricotta hotcakes with honeycomb butter, and sweet corn fritters with roast tomato, spinach and bacon.
✉ **433 Liverpool St (4, E5)** ☎ **9360 9631**
🕐 **Mon-Sat 7.30am-3pm ♿ yes**

Burgerman $
Hamburger Joint
Modern burgers served in an ultra mod interior (*Clockwork Orange* meets hi-tech Tokyo). Barbecued offerings include chicken fillet burgers with roasted capsicum, rocket and tomato relish. Add a serve of fries, and it's the perfect cheap eat.
✉ **116 Surrey St (4, E4)** ☎ **9361 0268** 🕐 **12-10pm ♿ yes**

Fez $$
Middle Eastern
Fez is always pulsing. Sit outside on cushion-covered benches or beneath the antique brass lanterns inside – either way, it's easy to be impressed by the fusion of North African ingredients and fresh local produce. Mezze plates are always popular, as is the couscous 'royale'.
✉ **247 Victoria St (4, E4)** ☎ **9360 9581** 🕐 **Mon-Fri 8am-3pm & 6-10pm, Sat-Sun 8am-10.30pm ♿ yes**

Fishface $$$
Seafood
Perpetually busy, Fishface plates up innovative seafood in a small slip of a space. To get an idea of what the fuss is about, try the tempura of whiting with cucumber pickle and pepper jam. The crème brûlée with stewed rhubarb is also notable.
✉ **132 Darlinghurst Rd (4, E4)** ☎ **9332 4803**
🕐 **6-11pm (till 10pm Sun) ♿ no**

Govinda's $
Indian
Govinda's \$14.90 dinner/movie deal is a winner. Fill up at the vegetarian Indian buffet, then head upstairs to the cinema and catch a newish release.
✉ **112 Darlinghurst Rd (4, D4)** ☎ **9380 5155 (restaurant), 9360 7853 (cinema)** 🕐 **6-10pm** ♿ **no V**

Latteria $
Cafe
It might be next door to Bar Coluzzi, but it's a million miles away on the style spectrum. Latteria's stainless steel and dark wood industrial decor attracts an arty crowd. Expect good strong coffee and a variety of toasted sandwiches.
✉ **320 Victoria St (4, D4)** ☎ **9331 2914**
🕐 **5am-7.30pm ♿ yes**

Le Petit Creme $
French
Le Petit Creme specialises

in French breakfasts. Head there for huge bowls of café au lait, over-sized omelettes and sassy, Gallic service. Alternatively, grab a freshly baked croissant for on-the-go sustenance.
✉ **118 Darlinghurst Rd (4, D4)** ☎ 9361 4738 ⏲ 7am-3pm (from 8am Sun) ♿ yes

Oh! Calcutta! $$
Indian
Oh, that goat curry! This smallish, modern restaurant dishes up north Indian cuisine in a contemporary setting. Jazz plays as patrons tuck into tandoori quail and desserts like rasmalai – rosewater and cardamom-flavoured ricotta dumplings. Bookings advisable.
✉ **251 Victoria St (4, E4)** ☎ 9360 3650 ⏲ dinner 6-11pm, lunch Fri only 12-2.30pm ♿ no

ONDE $$
French
Culturally enriching, palate pleasing and cheap – no wonder Onde is always busy. Try the calves liver with a generous serve of frites on the side. It's sure to make you a fan.
✉ **346 Liverpool St (4, E5)** ☎ 9331 8749 ⏲ Mon-Thurs 5.30-11pm, Fri-Sat 5.30-11.30pm, Sun 5.30-10pm ♿ no

Sel & Poivre $$
This French bistro rates highly with devoted regulars who swear by the simply prepared traditional dishes. Favourites include pepper steak with frites and a killer tarte Tatin. Bookings advisable at night.
✉ **263 Victoria St (4, E4)** ☎ 9361 6530 ⏲ 7am-10.30pm ♿ no

Tropicana $
Cafe
The Trop, (as it's fondly referred to) is the second home to out-of-work actors, travellers and taxi drivers. Follow their lead and take a seat in the large, undecorated room, drink endless cups of coffee and watch European soccer on TV. The food is an afterthought.
✉ **227b Victoria St (4, D4)** ☎ 9360 9809 ⏲ 5.30am-midnight ♿ yes

Simon Bracken

Healthy fare with Japanese flair at Glebe's Iku Wholefood

EAST SYDNEY

Bill & Toni's $
Italian
Still packed after all these years, Bill & Toni's serves inexpensive, conservative Italian staples. A $15 meal in the upstairs restaurant consists of entree, main, salad and a soft drink. It's a deal many Sydneysiders try to keep to themselves.
✉ **74 Stanley St (4, D2)** ☎ 9331 3497 🚍 Central ⏲ cafe: 7am-midnight; restaurant: lunch 12-2.30pm, dinner 6-10pm ♿ yes

GLEBE

The Boathouse on Blackwattle Bay $$$$
Seafood
The Boathouse offers 'alternative' harbour views of the Glebe Island bridge and industrial jetties. Bold offerings from the kitchen include eel terrine and steamed Moreton Bay scallops. Book ahead.
✉ **end of Ferry Rd (2, H8)** ☎ 9518 9011 🚍 431, 433 ⏲ Tues-Sun lunch 12-3pm, dinner 6.30-10.30pm ♿ yes

Iku Wholefood $
Vegetarian
Japanese influenced macrobiotic snacks and meals. Daily specials like asparagus tart with sea vegetables are supplemented by lentil burgers and nori rolls. The cute courtyard garden is great for lunch.
✉ **25a Glebe Point Rd (2, H8)** ☎ 9692 8720 🚍 431-4 ⏲ Mon-Fri 11am-9pm, Sat 11am-8.30pm, Sun 12-8pm ♿ no **V**

Bring Your Own
Many restaurants advertise that they're BYO, which stands for 'Bring Your Own'. This means you can bring your own alcohol to the restaurant, though you will usually be charged a corkage fee (around $2 per bottle). Most BYO eateries are unlicensed, but some licensed places also allow you to BYO, but it could be restricted to beer.

KINGS CROSS

Bayswater Brasserie $$$
Mod Oz
The crowd, the position and the food – Bayswater Brasserie continues to impress after almost 20 years. A good start is goat's cheese salad, followed by barbecued Barossa chicken. At night, enjoy cocktails in the courtyard bar.
✉ 32 Bayswater Rd (4, C5) ☎ 9357 2177 🚇 Kings Cross 🚌 330, 323-7, 365, 366, 387, L24 ⏰ Mon-Sat noon-11pm ♿ yes

LEICHHARDT

Bar Italia $
Italian
Bar Italia pumps. Leichhardt locals praise the faultless coffee, eccentric waiters and authentic Italian snacks. Queue for a table at dinner or dash in for home made gelati and biscotti during the day.
✉ 169 Norton St (2, H7) ☎ 9560 9981 🚌 435-40 ⏰ Mon-Thurs 9am-midnight, Fri-Sun 10am-1am ♿ yes

Elio $$$
Italian
Leichhardt's Little Italy is paved with bistros serving unadventurous fare. Elio's rises above the fray with its modern decor and inventive but homey dishes. The short, well considered menu features offerings like sardine fillets on grilled polenta. Bookings advised.
✉ 159 Norton St (2, H7) ☎ 9560 9129 🚌 435-40 ⏰ Mon-Sat dinner 6-10.30pm, Sun lunch 12-3pm ♿ yes

MANLY

Cafe Tunis $$
Tunisian
Authentic Tunisian food served on Manly's beachfront? Cafe Tunis is just one of the fantastic multicultural dining experiences Sydney offers. Try spiced fruit with sheep's yoghurt for breakfast and head back later in the day for the vegetarian couscous. Bookings advised.
✉ 30 Sth Steyne St (2, B14) ☎ 9976 2805 🚌 Wynyard, then bus 171, E69 or E71 ⛴ Manly ⏰ 7am-10pm ♿ yes V

NEWTOWN

La Kilimanjaro $$
African
Who would have thought that African cuisine would be such a hit in Sydney? La Kilimanjaro started the trend, serving authentic and fusion dishes to an appreciative audience. Spicy Senegalese chicken with couscous is a highlight.
✉ 280 King St (2, J8) ☎ 9557 4565 🚌 Newtown 🚌 423, 426, 428, L23 ⏰ lunch 12-3pm, dinner 6-10pm ♿ yes

Steki Taverna $$
Greek
Steki Taverna can't help but be fun. What with the Greek jazz band, authentic Mediterranean food and lots of dancing, it practically invented the word. Bookings advisable on weekends.
✉ 2 O'Connell St (2, J8) ☎ 9516 2191 🚌 Newtown 🚌 423, 426, 428, L23 ⏰ Wed-Fri 6.30-10.30pm, Sat-Sun 6.30-11.30pm ♿ yes

(L) Scouring Elio's innovative Italian menu (R) Newtown's eclectic offerings

PADDINGTON

To get to Oxford St and its surrounds, catch bus 378, 380, 382 or L82.

Arthur's Pizza $$
Italian

Arthur's fresh ingredients, seasonal menu and groovy locale have made it almost too popular. Pizza lovers cram inside the dark, wooden room and munch the night away. Try the Big Blue, a seafood pizza with marinated octopus, prawns and basil.
✉ 260 Oxford St (4, H6) ☎ 9331 1779 ⏰ Mon-Fri 5pm-midnight, Sat-Sun noon-midnight ♿ no

Buon Ricordo $$$$
Italian

Remember back in the old days, when the local restaurateur knew you so well that you let him choose your meal? Well, it's still happening at Buon Ricordo. Enter this buzzing osteria, and let chef Armando decide whether you need the roast spatchcock or the salmon carpaccio. Reservations essential.
✉ 108 Boundary St (4, F5) ☎ 9360 6729 ⏰ lunch Fri-Sat 12-2.30pm, dinner Tues-Sat 6.30-11pm ♿ no

Grand National $$$
Mod Oz Pub

Forget the classic counter meal. The Grand National is at the forefront of Sydney's pub revolution. Expect sophisticated dishes served in an Art Deco setting. Desserts are a winner – be sure to try the chocolate and honeycomb parfait. Bookings advisable.
✉ 161 Underwood St (4, J8) ☎ 9363 4557 ⏰ lunch Thurs-Sat 12-3pm, dinner Tues-Sat 6-10.30pm ♿ no

Paddington Inn $$
Mod Oz Pub

Recently renovated, the Paddo now serves well priced bistro fare in 2 funky rooms. Order beer battered fish & chips at the bar, slide into a comfortable booth and watch the surrounding social whirl.
✉ 338 Oxford St (4, H7) ☎ 9380 5277 ⏰ lunch 12-3pm, dinner 6-10pm ♿ no

Food Courts

Food courts are convenient places to grab a snack or a quick, inexpensive meal. Often located in shopping plazas and at the base of office high-rises, food courts offer takeaway meals from most corners of the globe. The food outlets are typically clustererd around a large eating area; you just buy what you want and try to find a seat. Hot Chinese, Thai and Indian meals are often available, as well as pizzas, burgers, fish & chips and ice cream. Increasingly, you can also get gourmet sandwiches, health food and sushi. Find food courts in these city shopping centres:

Queen Victoria Building 455 George St (3, K5)
Skygarden 77 Castlereagh St (3, K6)
Chifley Plaza 2 Chifley Square (3, H7)
Centrepoint cnr Castlereagh & Market Sts (3, K6)

Glenn Beanland

Shop till you drop and then refuel at the Queen Victoria Building's fine food court.

POTTS POINT

To get to Potts Point, take a train to Kings Cross, or catch bus 330, 323-7, 365, 366, 387 or L24.

Cafe Hernandez $
Cafe
Need a 4am coffee fix? Better find Cafe Hernandez. Tucked away from the Cross' main drag, it serves Spanish pastries and potent coffee day in, day out. Its rustic charm – an old piano, antique light fittings and kitsch oil paintings – appeals to students, night owls and cabbies.
✉ 60 King Cross Rd (4, D5) ☎ 9331 2343 ⏰ 24 hours ♿ no

Morans $$$
Mod Oz
This modern, elegant restaurant is the backdrop for chef Richard Purdue's self-assured menu. Flavours from Asia, Europe and the antipodes are artfully combined to create dishes like fig stuffed quail with de puy lentils. Those on a budget can fill up on superior breakfasts at the cafe next door.
✉ 61-63 Macleay St (4, A5) ☎ 9356 2223 ⏰ lunch Wed-Fri 12-3pm, dinner daily 6.30-11pm (till 10pm Sun) ♿ no

Odeon $$$
Mod Oz
The Odeon's curvy, Art Deco dining room is a choice location for business lunches and dinners. Slip into a leather booth, order the sour cream waffles and start dealing. Book ahead.
✉ 32 Orwell St (4, B5) ☎ 9331 0172 ⏰ Mon-Thurs 6.30-10.30pm, Fri noon-10.30pm, Sat-Sun 8am-10.30pm ♿ yes

Paramount $$$$
Mod Oz
Christine Manfield is Sydney's crown queen of Mod-Oz cuisine. Her slick dining room is always abuzz and the kitchen responds with fresh, confidently prepared dishes. The yellowfin tuna tartare with a nori omelette and wasabi flying fish roe is a must. Bookings essential.
✉ 73 Macleay St (4, A5) ☎ 9358 1652 ⏰ 6.30-11pm ♿ no

Potts Point locals adore Spring Espresso Bar.
Simon Bracken

Spring Espresso Bar $
Cafe
What this tiny, hole in the wall cafe lacks in size it makes up for in popularity. Sit among Potts Point hoi polloi and snack on pastries, panini and pies. If it's full, try **La Buvette** (☎ 9358 5113) next door, which has similar design, menu, prices and patrons.
✉ 65 Macleay St (4, A5) ☎ 9331 0190 ⏰ 7am-7pm ♿ yes

REDFERN

Casapueblo $$
South American
The flavours of Chile, Brazil, Peru and Uruguay unite at Casapueblo. The crumbed mussels with chilli and pork with lime and cashews are standout dishes. Bookings advisable.
✉ 650 Bourke St (2, J10) ☎ 9319 6377 ⏹ Central ⏹ 372 ⏰ Tues-Sat 6-10.30pm ♿ yes

ROSE BAY

Pier $$$$
Seafood
Perched over Rose Bay like a pelican about to take flight, Pier serves exhilarating seafood dishes, such as a ravioli of blue swimmer crab in consommé. All meals are cooked with brio and skill. Reservations essential.
✉ 594 New South Head Rd (2, G13) ☎ 9327 4187 ⏹ Bondi Junction, then bus 321 ⏹ 323-5, L24 ⏰ 12-3pm & 6-10pm (till 9pm Sun) ♿ no

ROZELLE

Tetsuya's $$$$
French/Japanese
A visit to Tetsuya's is considered by many to be the ultimate dining experience. Book way ahead to sample this exquisite, inspired French-Japanese fusion cuisine. Dishes like confit of ocean trout almost have their own fan club. Book 6 weeks ahead for Friday and Saturday.
✉ 729 Darling St (2, G7) ☎ 9555 1017 ⏹ X40, 440, 445-6 ⏰ lunch Tues-Sat 12-2.30pm, dinner Tues-Fri 7pm-midnight ♿ no

SURRY HILLS

To get to Surry Hills, catch the train to Central; from there it's a short stroll east.

Abdul's $
Middle Eastern
Locals praise Abdul's for its great big serves of baba ganauje (eggplant dip) and falafel. Gruff service is almost as legendary as the belly dancers on Saturday nights. Book for weekends.
✉ **563 Elizabeth St (2, J10) ☎ 9698 1275** ⏰ **Mon-Wed & Sun 10am-midnight, Thurs-Sat 10am-2am** ♿ **yes**

Cafe Niki $
Cafe
Gorgeous, grungy musicians and chattering academics make up the mix at the French-style Cafe Niki. Tiled walls, marble-topped tables and wooden benches are the setting for large serves of soup, salad and pasta.
✉ **544 Bourke St (4, K2) ☎ 9319 7517** ⏰ **Mon-Fri 7am-10pm, Sat 8am-10pm, Sun 8am-4pm** ♿ **yes**

Dolphin Hotel $$
Mod Oz
The jazzed up Dolphin, catering to Surry Hill's burgeoning bourgeoisie, does a neat line in lunch; a 'Modern Australian' yum cha. Table-side treats include venison carpaccio and seared scallops with halloumi. Book ahead.
✉ **412 Crown St (4, H1) ☎ 9331 4800** ⏰ **lunch 12-3pm, dinner 6-10pm (Sun till 9pm)**

Fatima's $
Lebanese
In a row of lookalike Lebanese restaurants, Fatima is the queen. Customers are treated to private cushion rooms, belly dancers and mammoth serves of inexpensive food. Particularly good are the crunchy falafel, garlic potatoes and mixed grill. Book for weekends.
✉ **296 Cleveland St (2, J10) ☎ 9698 4895** ⏰ **10am-3am** ♿ **yes**

Fuel $$$
Mod Oz
Size up an Aston Martin or Lotus while choosing between venison pie, a hearty sirloin steak or melt-in-the-mouth gnocchi. This relaxed, friendly bistro in a car showroom also has luscious desserts and a gourmet mini mart.
✉ **476-488 Crown St (4, J1) ☎ 9383 9388** ⏰ **Mon-Fri 12-3pm, Sat-Sun 8am-3pm, dinner daily 6.30-10pm** ♿ **no**

Longrain $$
Noodle Bar
Longrain makes serving hundreds of famished, fussy diners look easy. Housed in a century-old printing press, Longrain is packed with style-meisters snacking chef Martin Boetz's Thai-inspired delicacies. Sydney's other superstar chefs look on with envy and astonishment.
✉ **85 Commonwealth St (3, O7) ☎ 9280 2888** 🚉 **Central** ⏰ **lunch: Tues-Fri 12-2.30pm, dinner: Tues-Sun 6pm-11pm** ♿ **yes** **V**

Mohr Fish $$
Seafood
Reminiscent of an eel and mash shop in London's East End, Mohr Fish delivers quality seafood to a loyal clientele. Fill up on a bouillabaisse or tuna with pesto potatoes.
✉ **202 Devonshire St (4, K1) ☎ 9318 1326** ⏰ **10am-10pm** ♿ **yes**

Prasit's Northside Thai Takeaway $$
Thai
Prasit's cheap and cheerful decor belies the skill of the Thai chefs manipulating the woks. Hordes of hungry diners line up for exceptional dishes like banana flower salad, tofu tamarind and black sticky rice pudding.
✉ **395 Crown St (4, H1) ☎ 9332 1792** ⏰ **Tues-Sun 12-3pm & 5.30-10pm** ♿ **yes**

Simon Bracken

Shift your taste buds into first gear at Fuel.

THE ROCKS

To get to The Rocks, catch a train, bus or ferry to Circular Quay.

Bel Mondo $$$$
Italian

In Sydney's culinary hall of fame the Manfredi family hold top honours. Expect northern Italian cuisine perfectly executed in dramatic surrounds. For a more relaxed meal, sit at the antipasto bar and watch Stefano Manfredi direct meals from the pass. Bookings essential.
✉ L3, The Argyle Stores, 18-24 Argyle St (3, E6) ☎ 9241 3700 ⏰ restaurant: lunch Mon-Fri 12-2.30pm, dinner daily 6.30-10.30pm; bar: Mon-Fri noon-11pm, Sat 6-11pm, Sun 12-10pm ♿ no

Rockpool $$$$
Mod Oz

Neil Perry's modern seafood menu continues to wow the critics. For the past decade, Rockpool has held the toque of Sydney's best restaurant, and no element of this well-oiled operation fails to impress. Expect well executed contemporary cuisine with strong Asian influences, faultless service and an impressive wine list. It's worth the 35min wait for the passionfruit soufflé. Bookings essential.
✉ 107 George St (3, E6) ☎ 9252 1888 ⏰ lunch Mon-Fri 12-2.30pm, dinner Mon-Sat 6-11pm ♿ no

Sailors Thai Canteen $$$
Thai

Tuck into some of the best Thai food this side of Bangkok. Sit at a long, communal stainless steel table with arts-community grandees, politicians and media mavens and order the som dam (green papaya, peanut and dried prawn salad) and crispy oyster pancake. Try to score a balcony table, overlooking Circular Quay.
✉ 106 George St (3, E6) ☎ 9251 2466 ⏰ 12-8pm ♿ yes

VAUCLUSE

Vaucluse House Tearooms $
Afternoon Tea

Housed in a 1940s garden pavilion, set among 27 acres of sub-tropical gardens and overlooking a 19th-century mansion, the tearooms do a roaring trade in freshly baked scones and cakes.
✉ Vaucluse House, Wentworth Rd (2, F13) ☎ 9388 8188 🚌 325 ⏰ Tues-Sun 10am-4.30pm ♿ yes

WATSONS BAY

Doyles on the Beach $$$
Seafood

The quintessential Sydney dining experience – catch a ferry to Watsons Bay wharf for a seafood lunch at Doyles. Sit on the balcony of a 19th-century terrace house overlooking Sydney Harbour and tuck into a crustacean platter. Bookings advisable.
✉ 11 Marine Pde (2, F14) ☎ 9337 2007 🚌 324-5, L82 ⛴ Watsons Bay ⏰ lunch 12-3pm, dinner 6-9.30pm ♿ yes

WOOLLAHRA

Bistro Moncur $$$
French Brasserie

Mini moguls and ladies who lunch while away the afternoon at this modern, noisy, bistro. Gallic must-haves include French onion soufflé and roast duck with glazed turnips. The comprehensive, antipodean wine list is an extra thrill. Moncur's new sister establishment, **Bistro Deux** (☎ 9555 7788), 599 Darling St, Rozelle (2, G7) plates up similar fare.
✉ 116 Queen St (4, K10) ☎ 9363 2782 🚌 Edgecliff 🚌 378, 380, 382, L82 ⏰ lunch Tues-Sun 12-3pm, dinner Mon-Sat 6-10.30pm, Sun 6-9pm ♿ yes

The Centennial $$$
Pub

Wood-fired wonders for Woollahra luvvies. The Centennial's bright, white dining room is constantly abuzz with the lithe and chic, munching on roasted vegetable salads and snazzy, seafood pizzas. Bookings accepted for lunch only.
✉ 88 Oxford St (2, H11) ☎ 9362 3838 🚌 Bondi Junction 🚌 355, 378, 380, 382, L82 ⏰ 12-3pm, 6-10.30pm (till 9pm Sun) ♿ yes

WOOLLOOMOOLOO

Harry's Cafe de Wheels (4, A4) $

Takeaway Cafe

Harry's famous pea and pie floaters have fed cab drivers, marines and famished night owls for over 50 years. Sit on a milk crate overlooking hulking warships and gulp down a 'Tiger' (pie, peas, mashed potatoes and gravy).

✉ Cowper Wharf Rd ☎ 9357 3074 🚇 Kings Cross 🚌 311 🕐 Sun-Thurs 7.30am-1am, Fri-Sat 9am-4am ♿ yes

Simon Bracken

Hearty late-night eats

Tony Pyrzakowski's mural sets the mood at Harry's.

Waterside Treats

For great views and food by the beach, head to **Le Kiosk** (☎ 9977 4122), 1 Marine Pde, Shelly Beach, Manly (2, B14), which does good seafood.

Harbourside restaurants of note include: **Nielsen Park Kiosk** (☎ 9337 1574), Greycliffe Ave, Vaucluse (2, F13), which dishes out homemade pasta and seafood; **Quay** (☎ 9251 5600), Upper Level, Overseas Passenger Terminal, Circular Quay (3, D7) and **Wharf Restaurant** (☎ 9251 5600), Pier 4, Hickson Rd, Walsh Bay (3, C5), both serving Mod Oz cuisine; and **Merrony's** (☎ 9247 9323), 2 Albert St, Circular Quay (3, F7), a high-end French restaurant.

See the next page for more outstanding views.

WORTH A TRIP

Beach Road Restaurant $$$

Seafood

Don't let the bright and beachy atmosphere fool you, this destination restaurant plates up some spectacular Asian-inspired seafood. Enjoy an afternoon on Palm Beach afterwards.

✉ **1 Beach Rd, Palm Beach (1, A9)** ☎ **9974 1159** 🚇 **Town Hall, then bus L90 or 190** 🕐 lunch Fri-Sun 12-3pm, dinner Wed-Sun 7-10pm ♿ yes

Cleopatra $$$$

French

Upmarket French-Provençal food served in glorious surrounds. A guesthouse is available for those wanting to make a night of it. Bookings essential.

✉ **118 Cleopatra St, Blackheath (1, A3)** ☎ **4787 8456** 🚇 **Blackheath (Mt Victoria/Lithgow line from Central)** 🕐 lunch Sun 1-3pm, dinner 7.30-10pm ♿ no

Jonah's $$$$

Mediterranean

Perched high on a clifftop overlooking Whale beach, Jonah's prepares smart modern Mediterranean dishes (such as porcini mushroom risotto with sweet potato crisps) for an appreciative audience. Bookings advisable.

✉ **69 Bynya Rd, Palm Beach (1, A9)** ☎ **9974 5599** 🚇 **Town Hall, then bus L90 or 190** 🕐 lunch 12-2.30pm, dinner 6.30-10.30pm, breakfast Sat-Sun 8.30-10am ♿ yes

OUTSTANDING VIEWS

Given Sydney's stupendous setting, it's not surprising that it offers some seriously good combinations of food and views.

Bathers Pavilion $-$$$$
French/Asian

Impressive architecture (a 1920s Spanish Mission style pavilion), amazing views (Balmoral's sparkling beach) and outstanding food (deftly cooked French-Asian inspired dishes) collide to make Bathers' one of Sydney's most popular restaurants.

✉ 4 The Esplanade, Balmoral (2, D12) ☎ 9969 5050 🚊 Taronga Park Zoo, then bus 238 ⏰ cafe: 7am-10.30pm; restaurant: lunch 12-2.30pm, dinner 6.30pm-10.30pm ♿ yes

Blackwattle Canteen $
Mod Oz

Artists, bohemians and family groups head to Blackwattle for huge breakfasts and hearty lunches. The inexpensive food is not the only draw – water views and glimpses of both the Pyrmont and Harbour bridges are added allure. Booking recommended at weekends.

✉ 465 Glebe Point Rd, Glebe (2, G8) ☎ 9552 1792 🚌 431 ⏰ 8am-4pm (from 9am Sat-Sun) ♿ yes

Catalina $$$$
Mod Oz

Catalina's idyllic outlook over Sydney Harbour is hard to beat. Sit on the veranda watching seaplanes land and snack on freshly shucked rock oysters. Bookings essential.

✉ 1 Sunderland Ave

(next to Rose Bay ferry wharf) Rose Bay (2, G13) ☎ 9371 0555 🚉 Bondi Junction, then bus 321 🚌 323-5, L24 from Circular Quay ⏰ 12-10pm ♿ no

Forty One $$$$
Mod Oz

Oh those views! Failed mogul Alan Bond once earmarked this space as his private penthouse. Now, educated diners, mini-millionaires and sweaty-palmed men about to propose ascend the lift to sample complex and imaginative cuisine. Book ahead.

✉ L41, Chifley Tower, 2 Chifley Square (3, H7) ☎ 9221 2500 🚉 Martin Place ⏰ lunch Sun-Fri 12-3pm, dinner Mon-Sat 6-10pm ♿ no

Sean's Panaroma $$$
Mod Oz

Scenic ocean views, funky mix 'n' match furniture and huge, home-style breakfasts ensure that Sean's is always packed. Nighttime sees elegant dishes like preserved duck with figs being served. Bookings advisable.

✉ 270 Campbell Pde, North Bondi (2, H14) ☎ 9365 4924 🚉 Bondi Junction, then bus 380, 382 or L82 ⏰ breakfast/lunch Sat-Sun 9am-3.30pm, dinner Wed-Sat 6.30-10pm ♿ no

The Summit $$$$
Mod Oz

Sky-high views and prices are the ticket at The Summit,

a revolving restaurant with interior design inspired by Stanley Kubrick's *2001: A Space Odyssey*. Meals are Mod Oz with a rich, meaty French influence. Get giddy at the Orbit Bar afterwards.

✉ L47, Australia Sq (3, G6) ☎ 9247 9777 🚉 Wynyard ⏰ lunch 12-3pm, dinner 6pm-late (Sun buffet only); bar 5pm-late ♿ yes

(Top) Sean's Panaroma
(Bottom) The Summit

entertainment

Sydney adores the theatre and the concert hall, but it loves the beach even more. Often accused by other states of hedonism (to the point of anti-intellectualism), Sydneysiders merely shrug and apply some more suntan oil.

Sure, locals have season subscriptions to Opera Australia, the Sydney Theatre Company and Sydney Symphony Orchestra, but with so much sun, it's difficult to stay indoors for such serious pursuits. Consequently, the city's major arts companies concentrate on populist rather than more erudite works. It also means Sydney attracts a plethora of touring West End musicals, Andrew Lloyd Webber's especially.

The city boasts a multitude of after-dark venues, from stylish clubs to outdoor cinemas and live music pubs. Gay and lesbian culture informs much of Sydney's entertainment scene, with nightly drag shows, annual queer film festivals and regular dance parties.

Where to Go

Most of Sydney's entertainment venues are in the following areas:

City Centre & The Rocks – concert halls and mainstream theatres

Kings Cross & Redfern – smaller fringe dance and theatre companies

Oxford St, Darlinghurst & King St, Newtown – late-night cafes and gay and lesbian bars and clubs

Newtown, Surry Hills & Balmain – pubs featuring live rock, blues and jazz bands on a nightly basis

Potts Point, Darlinghurst & Paddington – nightclubs, hip bars

Just the Ticket

Tickets for shows can usually be purchased directly from the venue. Alternatively, Ticketek (☎ 9266 4800) offers credit card bookings (service fees are around $3 per ticket). A Halftix booth, located at the upper end of Martin Place, sells unsold tickets at half price on the day of the performance.

In the Know

Pick up the 'Metro' section in Friday's *Sydney Morning Herald* for comprehensive cinema, theatre and music listings. Free weekly street magazines like *On the Street* and *Revolver* specialise in band and club information.

Free Fun

Free entertainment proliferates during the summer months with jazz, classical and opera performances in the parks. January's Sydney Festival (p. 92) offers an abundance of outdoor events; check media for dates.

The weekend markets are great places to see buskers, mimes and street theatre, as are busy tourist precincts such as Circular Quay, Martin Place Amphitheatre, Kings Cross and Pitt St Mall. On Sunday, Speaker's Corner in the Domain is alive with debate as those who want to vent their spleen rant and rave to a crowd of curious onlookers and hecklers.

What's On

January *Sydney Festival* – see page 92
Australia Day – 26 Jan; Tall Ships race, regatta, fireworks
Big Day Out – music mosh at Homebush
Chinese New Year – Jan/Feb; dragon boat races in Darling Harbour, food stalls, fireworks, dances, acrobats, buskers, parade in Chinatown

February *Gay & Lesbian Mardi Gras* – see page 97-8
Tropfest – see page 97

March *Women's Festival* – a day of celebration and rabble-rousing to coincide with International Women's Day
Royal Easter Show – Mar/Apr; 12-day event held at Homebush which traditionally begins with a parade of country animals; has a distinctly agricultural flavour, but there's plenty to entertain city slickers

April *Festival of Fools* – starts 1 Apr; comedy capers, street performers, outdoor films, Fools Gala at the Town Hall

May *Sydney Writers Festival* – mid to late May

June *Sydney Film Festival* – mid to late June; held at the magnificent State Theatre, you can subscribe to the whole season or buy tickets (☎ 9660 3844) to individual screenings
Sydney Biennale – held in even years; international arts festival at the Art Gallery of NSW and other city venues

August *Sydney City to Surf* – 2nd Sunday in Aug; run from Hyde Park to Bondi Beach with around 20,000 competitors

September *Festival of the Winds* – 2nd Sunday; a kite flying festival with a multicultural theme at Bondi Beach

October *Manly International Jazz Festival* – Labour Day weekend; 3 days of be bop, re bop and za ba de da
Sydney Comedy Festival – last 3 weeks of Oct; loads of international and local acts, including stand-up, theatre and events

December *Sydney to Hobart Yacht Race* – 26 Dec; Sydney Harbour is crowded with onlookers for the start of this gruelling race
New Years Eve – 31 Dec; huge fireworks display over Sydney Harbour; Darling Harbour and Circular Quay are popular viewing sites

Life's a whirl at the party of the year – Sydney's Gay & Lesbian Mardi Gras.

BARS & PUBS

The Cricketers Arms

This Art Nouveau style pub hasn't yet fallen prey to the interior design craze that's hit most inner-city bars. It remains the favourite haunt of arts students, workers and travellers, attracted to inexpensive counter meals and good conversation.
✉ **106 Fitzroy St, Surry Hills (4, J3)** ☎ **9331 3301** 🚃 **Central** 🚌 **374** ⏰ **Mon-Sat noon-midnight, Sun 12-10pm**

Darlo Bar

A long sliver of a bar decorated with mix 'n' match retro stuff, it attracts inner-city arty types. Young filmmakers, writers and actors cruise, peruse and shmooze. Afterwards, they head to the **Green Park** (☎ 9380 5311), 360 Victoria St, Darlinghurst (4, E4), for a game of pool.
✉ **Royal Sovereign Hotel, 306 Liverpool St, Darlinghurst (4, E4)** ☎ **9331 3672** 🚃 **Kings Cross** 🚌 **330, 323-7, 365, 366, 387, L24** ⏰ **Mon-Sat 10am-midnight, Sun 12-10pm**

Lord Nelson Brewery Hotel – the city's oldest?

Simon Bracken

Hotel Bondi

This landmark hotel directly opposite Bondi Beach has seen major renovations. Locals and tourists now happily mingle in the 'Sand' and 'Bombora' bars, playing pool, listening to bands and drinking till the early hours.
✉ **178 Campbell Pde (2, H14)** ☎ **9130 3271** 🚃 **Bondi Junction, then bus 380, 382 or L82** ⏰ **10am-4am**

Lord Nelson Brewery Hotel

Built in 1842, the Lord Nelson claims to be Sydney's oldest pub. Go for a filling counter lunch (beef pie with mash and peas $7) and a robust beer from their micro-brewery.
✉ **19 Kent St, The Rocks (3, D4)** ☎ **9251 4044** 🚃 🚌 🚢 **Circular Quay** ⏰ **11am-11pm**

Old Fitzroy Hotel

Want a bit of culture and a bowl of curry? At the Old Fitzroy, $26 buys a Malaysian laksa, a beer and a ticket to the on-site theatre. Soon-to-be-famous thespians perform Pinter, Genet and new fringe pieces. Bookings advisable.
✉ **129 Dowling St, Woolloomooloo (4, C4)** ☎ **9356 3848, theatre 9294 4296** 🚃 **Kings**

Cool-a-bars

Check out the following slinky city bars:

Astral Bar (☎ 9777 9000), Star City Casino (p. 100)

Dug Out Bar & Lava Lounge (☎ 9331 3066), Burdekin Hotel, 2 Oxford St, Darlinghurst (4, E1)

Fix (☎ 9332 2566), Kirketon Hotel (p. 103), 229 Darlinghurst Rd, Darlinghurst (4, D4)

International Bar (☎ 9360 9080), 14th fl, 227 Victoria St, Darlinghurst (4, D4)

Lobby Lounge & Horizons Cocktail Lounge (☎ 9250 6000), ANA Hotel (p. 102)

Mint (☎ 9233 5388), 53 Martin Place (3, J7)

Orbit Bar (☎ 9247 9777), The Summit, Australia Square (p. 86)

Cross 🚌 311-12 🕐
Mon-Sat noon-
midnight, Sun 3-10pm

Paddington Inn
The trim, terrific and thirsty
all head to the Paddo on
Saturdays (after the market)
to flirt, gossip and people-
watch. As day turns to
night they adjourn to the
funky bistro for antipasto
and mezze plates.
✉ 338 Oxford St,
Paddington (4, H7)
☎ 9380 5277 🚌 378,
380, 382, L82 🕐 Mon-
Wed & Sun noon-
midnight, Thurs-Fri
noon-1am, Sat 11am-
1am

Pontoon
Pontoon looks like the type
of place that Vogue editors
try to keep secret; it's
modern, minimal and
marvellous. Luckily it's also
easy to find. Just look for
all the chilled-out business
types and tourists sitting on
low chairs under shade
umbrellas.
✉ North Promenade,
Cockle Bay Wharf,

Darling Harbour (3, L4)
☎ 9267 7099 🚇 Town
Hall, monorail, SLR 🚈
888 🚢 Darling Harbour
🕐 noon-2am

Slip Inn
During the week sharp
business boys and girls
gather to play pool, drink in
the courtyard bar and cut
deals in the hip bistro.
✉ 111 Sussex St (3, J4)
☎ 9299 2199 🚇
Martin Place, monorail
🚢 Darling Harbour 🕐
Mon-Fri noon-midnight,
Sat 6pm-midnight

Wine Banc
A sophisticated,
subterranean bar in which
to sip South Australian
sauvignon and snack on
steak frites. High prices
match the breadth and
depth of the wine list.
✉ Basement, 53
Martin Pl (enter via
Elizabeth St) (3, J7)
☎ 9233 5399 🚇
Martin Place 🕐 Mon-
Fri noon-midnight, Sat
6pm-midnight

DANCE CLUBS

ARQ
If Noah had to fill his boat
with groovy and gay-friendly
night clubbers, he'd
definitely head to ARQ for
Saturday night's 'Promised
Land'. Comprising a cocktail
bar, restaurant, oyster/wine
bar, recovery room and 2
dance-floors, ARQ makes it
easy to stay until you don't
know what day it is.
✉ 16 Flinders St,
Darlinghurst (4, F2)
☎ 9380 8700 🚌 380,
378 🕐 Mon-Fri noon-
2am, Sat-Sun 24 hours
💲 Fri $10, Sat $15,
free other nights

The Cave
Casino high-rollers and
stylish young things head
to the Cave. It's a sure bet
that in between all the
high-tech lasers and plush
velvet you'll be paying sky-
high prices for drinks.
✉ Star City Casino,
Pirrama Rd, Pyrmont (3,
J1) ☎ 9566 4755 🚇
Town Hall or Central,
then SLR 🚌 443, 888,
Star City buses 🚢
Pyrmont Bay 🕐 Wed-
Sun 9pm-5am

Club 77
Talented DJs Phil Smart and
Sugar Ray rule the roost at
77, a small club devoted to
experimental dance music.
Thursday night's popular
Club Kooky sees cyber-
punks, queer ferals and
techno-freaks getting
trancey and tribal.
✉ 77 William St, East
Sydney (4, C2) ☎ 9361
4981 🚇 Kings Cross
🚌 330, 323-27, 365-
66, 387, L24 🕐 Wed-
Sun 10pm-4am

Pub Scenes
Pubs and bars are an important part of Sydney's
social scene. Try going to a few during the week
because they often have a totally different
atmosphere to the weekends when the roving
hordes are out on the town.

Pubs vary from the traditional with their tiled
walls to the modern, stylish Art Deco bar. They are
often multi-purpose and many now have the
ubiquitous poker machines and betting; most
serve food and some have a variety of live
entertainment.

Other notable pubs include the **Four in Hand** (☎
9326 2254), 105 Sutherland St (4, G9), and **Grand
National** (☎ 9363 4557), 161 Underwood St (p.
81), in Paddington; and the **Light Brigade** (☎ 9331
2930), 2a Oxford St, in Woollahra (4, K9).

DCM

On the weekend, hard-core dance fans of all persuasions head to DCM. It's busiest after 5am, with Muscle Marys, drag queens and scantily clad clubbers crowding the dance floor and chill-out rooms. The enormous cloakroom lets patrons wear as much or as little as they like.

✉ L1, 33 Oxford St, Darlinghurst (4, E1) ☎ 9267 7380 ⏲ Fri & Sun 11pm-8am, Sat 10pm-9am

Home

A massive, purpose-built club, this 2000-capacity venue comprises a huge dance floor, outdoor balconies and secluded VIP rooms. Sunday night's 'Cocktails at Home' is the highlight of the week.

✉ Cockle Bay Wharf, Darling Harbour (3, L4) ☎ 9266 0600 🚊 Town Hall, monorail, SLR 🚌 888 ⛴ Darling Harbour ⏲ Fri-Sat 10pm-5am, Sun 6pm-midnight

Q Bar

Funky night-owls call in late to play pool, pinball and dance to hip-hop and deep house. The door policy can be tough on weekends, so dress accordingly.

✉ L2, 44 Oxford St, Darlinghurst (4, E1) ☎ 9360 1375 🚌 378, 380, 382, L82 ⏲ Mon-Thurs & Sun 5pm-5am, Fri-Sat 4pm-9am

Soho Bar & Velvet Lounge

Soho offers laid-back music and city skyline views, while Velvet Lounge downstairs focuses on funky beats for an 'upmarket dance' crowd – that means models and those who love them.

✉ 171 Victoria St, Potts Point (4, C4) ☎ 9358 6511 🚊 Kings Cross 🚌 330, 323-7, 365, 366, 387, L24 ⏲ bar & lounge: Fri-Sat 10pm-6am

ROCK, JAZZ & BLUES

The Basement

Sydney's premier jazz venue presents big touring acts (Herbie Hancock) and big local talent (Vince Jones). A broad musical mandate also sees funk, blues and soul bands performing. Avoid the standing-room only bar; it's best to book a table for stage views.

✉ 29 Reiby Pl, Circular Quay (3, F7) ☎ 9251 2797 🚊 🚌 ⛴ Circular Quay ⏲ Mon-Thurs noon-1.30am, Fri noon-2.30am, Sat 7.30pm-3am, Sun 7.30pm-1am ⑤ local acts around $12, international $27 ⚓ no

Empire Hotel

The Empire's public bar is the site of some of Sydney's best blues music. Local bands with loyal followings (The Mighty Reapers, Hippos and Foreday Riders) play free gigs. Look out for monthly steel guitar, country and Hawaiian music nights.

✉ cnr Parramatta Rd & Johnston St, Annandale (2, H7) ☎ 9557 1701 🚊 Central 🚌 438, 440, 461 ⏲ Mon-Sat 10am-midnight, Sun 10am-10pm ⚓ no

Enmore Theatre

Originally a vaudeville playhouse, the faded, somewhat charming Enmore now hosts local and international bands. The 1600 capacity theatre resembles an old cinema, with wooden floors, lounge areas and balconies.

✉ 132 Enmore Rd, Newtown (2, J8) ☎ 9550 3666 🚊 Newtown 🚌 423, 426, 428, L23 ⏲ box office Mon-Fri 9am-5pm, Sat 10am-2pm ⚓ school holiday events

Once a vaudeville playhouse, Enmore Theatre is now the place to see live rock.

The Excelsior Hotel

Most nights, the Excelsior has an array of local rock, blues, rockabilly and grunge acts. Quality may waiver but, hey, it's free. Close by is the **Hopetoun** (☎ 9361 5257), 416 Bourke St, Surry Hills (4, H2), a diminutive pub often crawling with record label scouts looking for the 'next big thing'. International acts sometimes play 'secret' gigs here.
✉ **64 Foveaux St, Surry Hills (4, H1)** ☎ **9211 4945** 🚇 **Central** ⏱ **Mon-Thurs 10am-midnight, Fri-Sat 10am-3am, Sun 10am-10pm** ⚲ **no**

The Globe

Popular local indie bands (The Whitlams, Jebediah, Superjesus) and mid-size internationals play to an informed rock crowd. Two purpose built rooms and low cover charges have made the Globe an increasingly busy venue since it opened in 1997.
✉ **379 King St, Newtown (2, J8)** ☎ **9519 0220** 🚇 **Newtown** 🚌 **422-3, 426, 428, L23** ⏱ **8pm-midnight (till 2am Fri-Sat)** ⚲ **no**

Harbourside Brasserie

The Harbourside Brasserie presents a regular roster of middle-of-the-road jazz, blues, cabaret and comedy acts. Sometimes a more exciting band slips through the net, especially during the Sydney Festival in January.
✉ **Pier 1, Hickson Rd, Walsh Bay (3, C6)** ☎ **9252 3000** 🚇 **Circular Quay** 🚌 **339, 431-4** ⏱ **6pm-2am** ⑤ **local acts around $10, international $25** ⚲ **yes**

The Metro

Many believe the Metro is Sydney's best rock venue. Big-name indie bands, well-chosen local acts and international DJs are the main draw. Theatre-style tiered seating, air conditioning, good sound and sight lines add to the attraction.
✉ **624 George St, Sydney (3, M5)** ☎ **9264 2666** 🚇 **Town Hall; Central** ⏱ **Mon-Fri 8pm-1am, Sat-Sun 11pm-7am** ⚲ **no**

See the big names at the Metro.

Simon Bracken

Rose, Shamrock & Thistle Hotel

Well-known blues and folk bands perform in this purpose-built auditorium also known as The Three Weeds. When it all gets too much, retire to the public bar for a beer and a game of pool.

✉ **193 Evans St, Rozelle (2, G7)** ☎ **9810 2244** 🚌 **Town Hall, then bus 500-2, 504, 506, 508 or 510** ⏱ **noon-midnight (till 10pm Sun)** ⚲ **no**

Soup Plus

Inner-city jazzniks cram into this basement restaurant to hear mostly mainstream jazz. Monday's jam sessions feature everything from trad to bop, and later in the week noisy office parties swing to contemporary rhythms. Bookings advised.
✉ **Basement Level, 383 George St, Sydney (3, J6)** ☎ **9299 7728** 🚇 **Town Hall** ⏱ **Mon-Sat noon-midnight** ⑤ **Mon-Thurs $5, Fri-Sat $20 (dinner & show)** ⚲ **yes**

Sydney Entertainment Centre

(3, N4) Sydney's largest indoor stadium venue holds over 12,000 screaming rock and pop fans. Past acts have included Janet Jackson, Bob Dylan and Pearl Jam. The interior lacks charm but provides adequate seating and sound – book ahead, especially for big names.
✉ **Harbour St, Haymarket** ☎ **9320 4200** 🚇 **Central, monorail, SLR** ⏱ **box office Mon-Fri 9am-5pm, Sat 10am-1pm** ⚲ **school holiday events**

Sydney Festival

Running for 3 weeks in January, Sydney's major arts and culture festival is organised around a theme or central aesthetic and then shoots out every which way into performance, visual art and 'happenings'. International and Australian performers run the gamut from opera to surreal gymnastics and water puppetry. Log on to www.sydneyfestival.org.au for details.

ABORIGINAL PERFORMANCE

Bangarra Dance Theatre

Only a decade old, Bangarra is widely regarded as Australia's finest Aboriginal dance company. Artistic director Stephen Page creates a fusion of the contemporary and the indigenous, blending traditional Torres Strait Islander dance with western technique. Bookings advisable.

✉ Pier 4/5 Hickson Rd, Walsh Bay (3, C5) ☎ 9251 5333 ⓡ Circular Quay ⚍ 339, 431-4, Matinee shuttle from Queen Victoria Building (Wed & Sat) ⓘ box office Mon-Fri 10am-6pm ♿ yes

Gavala

Gavala, an Aboriginal owned and run gallery/shop, holds traditional dance and didjeridu demonstrations. They also give informative talks on Aboriginal history and culture.

✉ L2, Harbourside Shopping Centre, Darling Harbour (3, L3) ☎ 9212 7232 ⓡ Town Hall, monorail, SLR ⚍ 888 ⓘ shop 10am-7pm, performances 4pm Mon, Wed & Sun ⑤ $5-10 ♿ yes

National Aboriginal & Islander Skills Development Association (N.A.I.S.D.A)

N.A.I.S.D.A holds mid and end of year dance shows for the public, showcasing the talent of their students. Call for program details and to book.

✉ 3 Cumberland St, The Rocks (3, D6) ☎ 9252 0199 ⓡ ⚍ ⚓ Circular Quay ⓘ call for details ♿ yes

For an insight into indigenous culture, attend a traditional Aboriginal performance.

CLASSICAL MUSIC, DANCE & OPERA

Conservatorium of Music

Closed for renovations until Jan 2001, the Conservatorium has relocated from the Botanical Gardens to new premises. However, its talented musical students (and their teachers) continue to provide recitals. The annual program includes choral, jazz, operatic and chamber pieces. Bookings advisable at night.

✉ Australian Technology Park, Garden St, Alexandria (2, J9) ☎ 9351 1222 ⓡ Redfern ⚍ 308-10 ♿ yes

Musical Recitals

The **Great Hall** (☎ 9351 2949) at Sydney University (2, H8) plays host to the highly regarded Chamber Choir, and the **John Clancy Auditorium** (☎ 9358 3471) at NSW University is home to the Australia Ensemble. Boasting near perfect acoustics, Sydney's large, new **City Recital Hall** (☎ 8256 2222) in Angel Place (3, H6) attracts top-flight chamber music ensembles and opera singers.

Some of Sydney's churches present a variety of classical music concerts and recitals. They include **St Andrew's Cathedral** (☎ 9265 1661), cnr George and Bathurst Sts (3, L5); **St James Church** (☎ 9232 3022), 173 King St (3, J7); **St Philip's Church** (☎ 9247 1071) on York St (3, G5) and **St Stephen's Church** (☎ 9221 1688) at 197 Macquarie St (3, H7). Call for program details.

The Domain

Each summer, thousands of Sydneysiders pack a picnic hamper and head to the Domain to enjoy a series of free twilight concerts. The 3 most popular are held in January: Opera Australia's *Opera in the Park* (☎ 9319 1088); Sydney Symphony Orchestra's *Symphony in the Domain* (☎ 9334 4644); and the Sydney Festival's *Jazz in the Domain* (☎ 8248 6500). The popular Carols by Candlelight concert is held in the Domain on Christmas Eve.
✉ **The Domain, Sydney (3, K9)** 🚉 **Martin Place; St James** 🚌 **411, 200** ♿ **yes**

Eugene Goosens Hall

This intimate hall is located at the Australian Broadcasting Corporation's headquarters. Be a (silent) member of a live musical broadcast, hear lectures by leading conductors or listen to the Sydney Symphony Orchestra recording a new CD. Synergy (☎ 9333 1600), Sydney's celebrated percussion ensemble, also performs at the hall. Bookings advisable.
✉ **700 Harris St, Ultimo (3, P4)** ☎ **9333 1500** 🚉 **Central, monorail, SLR** ⏲ **call for details**

One Extra Dance Company

This dynamic, contemporary dance company features young choreographers and dancers who concentrate on new Australian works. Bookings advisable.
✉ **The Seymour Centre, cnr City Rd & Cleveland St, Chippendale (2, H9)** ☎ **9364 9400** 🚉 **Redfern; Central** 🚌 **422, 423, 426, 428** ⏲ **Mon-Sat 9.30am-6.30pm**

The Performance Space

Russell Dumas' Dance Exchange (☎ 9357 3576) often performs spiky, modern dance pieces at this experimental theatre. His interest in developing a unique Australian dance style constantly challenges and intrigues. Bookings advisable.
✉ **199 Cleveland St, Redfern (2, J9)** ☎ **9319 5091, 9698 7235** 🚉 **Redfern; Central** 🚌 **372** ⏲ **office Mon-Fri 10am-6pm, box office open 1hr before show**

Sydney Opera House

(3, D9) See boxed text, above.
✉ **Bennelong Point, Circular Quay** ☎ **9250 7111/7777** 🚉 🚌 ⛴ **Circular Quay** ⏲ **box office Mon-Sat 9am-8.30pm** 💲 **concessions and standing room tickets available** ♿ **school holiday concerts**

Symphony in the Domain attracts thousands of music lovers each summer.

C. Moore Hardy (Sydney Festival)

THEATRE & COMEDY

Belvoir Street Theatre

Neil Armfield, the artistic director of Company B (as the Belvoir Street Company is now known) is the darling of the Sydney theatre world. Cinema stars like Geoffrey Rush and Cate Blanchett clamour to perform his adventurous interpretations of Chekhov, Shakespeare and Gogol. Bookings advisable.
✉ 25 Belvoir St, Surry Hills (2, H10) ☎ 9699 3444 ⛴ Central ⏰ box office Mon 9.30am-6pm, Tues-Sat 9.30am-7.30pm, Sun 2.30-7.30pm

The Bristol Arms

The Bristol Arms is 5 levels of fun including a pub, restaurant and nightclub. They also run twice weekly comedy nights. Rambunctious crowds enjoy local and international stand-up comedians, fun short films and the ever-popular open-mike section.
✉ 81 Sussex St, Sydney (3, J4) ☎ 9262 5491 ⛴ Wynyard ⏰ Wed & Fri 8pm ⑤ $10 ♿ no

The Comedy Store

Sydney's longest running comedy venue offers local stand-up acts and international names for an often rowdy crowd. Wednesday is open-mike night; performances range from exciting to execrable. Bookings advisable.
✉ Fox Studios, cnr Long Rd & Driver Ave, Moore Park (2, J11) ☎ 9564 3900 🚌 339 ⏰ Tues-Sun 5pm-12.30am ⑤ show $10-20, dinner & show $25-40 (no concession Fri-Sat)

Stables Theatre

(4, D4) Originally a 19th-century horse stable, this tiny space is now home to the Griffin Theatre Company. Widely acclaimed by critics, the company is dedicated to nurturing new writers and performing experimental works by contemporary Australian playwrights. Bookings advisable.
✉ 10 Nimrod St, Darlinghurst ☎ 9250 7799 ⛴ Kings Cross 🚌 330, 323-7, 365, 366, 387, L24 ⏰ box office Mon-Fri 9am-8.30pm ⑤ $22/17

State Theatre (3, K6)

The gloriously rococo State Theatre is just one of many inner-city venues showcasing West-End musicals, pop concerts and celebrity performances. Check newspapers for current shows. Bookings advisable.
✉ 4 Market St, Sydney ☎ 9373 6655; 1902 262 588 for recorded information ⛴ Town Hall; St James ⏰ Mon-Fri 9am-5.30pm

The Wharf Theatre

(3, C5) The modern Wharf complex, near The Rocks, comprises 2 theatres. The Sydney Theatre Company performs smaller and more experimental works in both venues. Bookings advisable. The on-site restaurant with harbour views is handy for a pre-theatre meal.
✉ Pier 4, Hickson Rd, Walsh Bay ☎ 9250 1700/1777 ⛴ Circular Quay 🚌 339, 431-4, Matinee shuttle from Queen Victoria Building (Wed & Sat) ⏰ box office Mon-Sat 9am-8.30pm ⑤ concession, standing room & matinee tickets available

Rococo splendour of the State Theatre

Play it Again

Major commercial theatres that host imported big-budget productions include the restored **Capitol** (☎ 9320 5000), 13 Campbell St, Haymarket (3, O5), **Her Majesty's Theatre** (☎ 9212 3411), 107 Quay St, Haymarket (3, P4) and the **Theatre Royal** (☎ 9202 2200), MLC Centre, King St, Sydney (3, J6).

Simon Bracken

CINEMAS

Academy Twin Cinema

Arthouse stalwarts are kept smiling by the consistently good selection of independent Australian and international releases. Just down the street is the **Verona Cinema** (☎ 9360 6099), 17 Oxford St, which screens similar fare. ✉ **3a Oxford St, Paddington (4, G3)** ☎ **9331 3457**, info line 9361 4453 🚌 378, 380, 382, L82 🕓 11am-9.30pm ⑤ $12/5-9, Mon $8

Chauvel Cinema

The Chauvel's double-feature programs focus on the highbrow, the cult and the quirky. Expect noir classics, early Australian gems and b&w masterpieces. ✉ **Paddington Town Hall, cnr Oatley Rd & Oxford St, Paddington (4, H6)** ☎ **9361 5398**

🚌 378, 380, 382, L82 🕓 1-9pm ⑤ $12/6-9, Mon & Tues $7.50

Dendy Cinema

From tart-house to arthouse, this former site of a Chinese porn cinema is now the established Dendy. Home of first-run, independent films from around the world, the cushy theatre is augmented by a popular bar and cafe. ✉ **19 Martin Pl (3, J7)** ☎ **9233 8166** 🚊 Martin Place 🕓 12.30-9pm ⑤ $12/7.50-9, Mon $7.50

Hoyts City Cinema

Hoyts is the largest, cleanest and most modern of the 3 mega-cinema chains lining this section of George St. Expect to see all the big American blockbusters and other mainstream fare. Bookings advisable. ✉ **505-23 George St,**

Sydney (3, M5) ☎ 9273 7460 🚊 Town Hall, monorail 🕓 Sun-Thurs 10am-10pm, Fri-Sat 10-1am ⑤ $12.50/8-9.50, Tues $7

IMAX Theatre (3, L4)

Sure, it's big bucks for a 45min movie, but then everything about IMAX is huge. The mega-large screen (8 storeys high) displays a selection of kid-friendly documentaries which manage to wow adults as well. ✉ **Southern Promenade, Darling Harbour** ☎ **9281 3300** 🌐 www.imax.com.au 🚊 Town Hall, monorail, SLR 🚌 888 🚢 Darling Harbour 🕓 Sun-Thurs 9.30am-10pm, Fri-Sat 9.30am-11pm ⑤ $14.95/11.95-12.95

Moonlight Cinema

Watching a movie under the stars is a blissful way to enjoy a balmy summer evening. Bring a rug, a picnic basket and a mate. The schedule includes faves like *Pulp Fiction*, *Blade Runner* and *Cinema Paradiso*. Bookings

The IMAX theatre's 8 storey screen makes movie-going a larger-than-life experience.

Simon Bracken

advisable; or buy tickets at the gate from 7.30pm. ✉ **Centennial Park Amphitheatre (entry via Woollahra Gate), Oxford St, Centennial Park (2, J11) ☎ 1900 933 899 screening details, 136 100 Ticketmaster 🚊 Bondi Junction 🚌 355, 378, 380, 382, L82 ⏰ late Nov-mid Feb 8.45pm ⑤ $12.50/8-9**

TropFest

Sydney's outdoor short film festival gets bigger every year. It's a made-to-order event – filmmakers must prepare their film within a very short time, and to prove that they're playing ball, they must include an item in their entry chosen by Tropfest shortly before the festival. Previous clues have included a coffee bean, a teaspoon and a kiss. Films (no longer than 7mins long) are screened in late February in the Domain and in cafes along Victoria St, Darlinghurst. Call ☎ 9368 0434 or log on to www.tropfest .com.au for more information.

GAY & LESBIAN SYDNEY

To get to all the following venues, catch bus 378, 380, 382 or L82.

The Albury Hotel
The Albury's claim to being gay Sydney's social epicentre holds some merit. Expect nightly drag shows, swooningly good-looking barmen and a hot, young crowd. ✉ **6 Oxford St, Paddington (4, G3) ☎ 9361 6555 ⏰ Mon-Sat 2pm-2am, Sun 2pm-midnight**

Barracks
Butch boys and leather clones gather at Barracks to play pool and then play with each other in the dungeon room. Early in the week the vibe is relaxed; Sunday's roast dinner is particularly homey. Friday and Saturday nights are very sweaty and sexy. ✉ **Taylor Square Hotel, 1-5 Flinders St, Darlinghurst (4, F2) ☎ 9360 6373 🚌 378, 380, 382, L82 ⏰ Mon-Sat 5pm-3am, Sun 4pm-midnight**

Beauchamp
The buzzy Beauchamp is always full of friendly, non-scene guys. A fave after-work haunt, the pub's cosy

Cabaret fun on Sydney's streets during the Mardi Gras

Greg Elms

decor is enhanced by spunky barmen and camp disco classics on the turntable. The Base Bar downstairs is more stylish and seductive. ✉ **267 Oxford St, Darlinghurst (4, G3) ☎ 9331 2575 🚌 378, 380, 382, L82 ⏰ Sun-**

Thurs noon-midnight, Fri-Sat noon-2am

Gilligans
Fashionable boys on the prowl start their night at Gilligan's cocktail lounge. Arrive early, grab a window seat, a Long Island Iced Tea and start flirting.

✉ Oxford Hotel, 134 Oxford St, Darlinghurst (4, F2) ☎ 9331 3467 ⏱ Sun-Tues 5pm-midnight, Wed-Thurs 5pm-1am, Fri-Sat 5pm-2am

Midnight Shift

Sydney's oldest and gayest club continues to pack in a varied clientele, from beefcakes to drags. With pool tables, bars and dance areas over 2 floors, the Shift remains a sociable and sexy destination.

✉ 85 Oxford St, Darlinghurst (4, E2) ☎ 9360 4319 ⏱ Mon-Thurs noon-5am, Fri-Sat noon-9am

Stonewall Hotel

A newer venue, but already a firm favourite. Three levels of bars and dance floors attract a cruisey, friendly crowd. Regular cabaret and games nights (drag shows, gay bingo, karaoke) add a tongue-in-cheek twist to the sophisticated space.

✉ 175 Oxford St, Darlinghurst (4, F2) ☎ 9360 1963 ⏱ Mon-Thurs noon-3am, Fri-Sun noon-5am

The Tool Shed

Need a ticket to a mega-dance party? Head to the Tool Shed, a centrally located sex shop and ticketing agent.
✉ 81 Oxford St, Darlinghurst (4, E2) ☎ 9332 2792 ⏱ 10am-2am

Mardi Gras

Sydney's Gay and Lesbian Mardi Gras is a month-long arts festival which culminates in a fantabulous parade and party. It's the largest arts festival of its kind in the world – events around town include parties, fairs, exhibitions, celebrations, commemorations, theatre, cabaret, cyberspace happenings, themed pool parties, debates, readings, discussions, music and dance.

The last Saturday in February is the culmination of Mardi Gras – it's parade night! Suddenly the gyms empty out, the hairdressers are deserted and you can't hire a costume for quids.

The parade begins on the corner of Elizabeth and Liverpool Sts around 7.30pm, and prances the length of Oxford St before trundling down Flinders St, Moore Park Rd and Driver Ave to the old Sydney Showgrounds. The traditional leader of the parade is the Dykes on Bikes – what comes next is anybody's guess but you can expect to see a lot of feathers, leather and glamorama as well as floats with more serious themes.

If you want to be among the 700,000 or so watching the parade, find some friends with a balcony view of Oxford St or set up with a milk crate on the road a few hours before it starts. It's a good idea to take some water with you.

Call the festival hotline (☎ 9266 4822) or check out the website at www.mardigras.com.au for details.

SPECTATOR SPORT

You'll find vocal crowds and world-class athletes in action on just about every weekend of the year in Sydney.

Football

Rugby League Sydney is one of the world capitals of rugby league. The main competition, run by the National Rugby League (NRL), is the Optus Cup, which includes interstate sides. Games are played at various grounds, but the sell-out finals are played in August/September at **Sydney Football Stadium** (☎ 9360 6601), Moore Park, Paddington (4, K5) and **Stadium Australia** (☎ 9266 4800), Homebush (2, F1). Tickets cost $15-$25.

The other big rugby league series is the State of Origin, played in Sydney, Brisbane and Melbourne. The NSW versus Queensland game generates a lot of passion.

Rugby Union The less brutal game of rugby union has a less fanatical following, but the Australian rugby union team, the Wallabies, are world-beaters. You can occasionally see them in action against international teams in Sydney.

Aussie Rules Aussie Rules football is a unique, exciting sport – only Gaelic football is anything like it. The Sydney Swans are Sydney's – and NSW's – only contribution to the Australian Football League, though Melbourne-based club the Kangaroos play some home games in Sydney now. Games are played at the 40,000-seat **Sydney Cricket Ground** (☎ 9360 6601) in Moore Park, Paddington (2, J11); tickets are $20-40. The football season runs through autumn and winter, from March to September.

Soccer Soccer is slowly gaining popularity, thanks in part to the success of the national team, the Socceroos, and to the high profile of some Aussies playing overseas. The national league is only semi-professional and games attract a relatively small following. In the past most clubs were ethnically based, but now they appeal to the broader community. Games are played at football grounds around the suburbs. For information, contact Soccer Australia (☎ 9267 0799).

Cricket
The **Sydney Cricket Ground** (2, J11) is the venue for sparsely attended Pura Milk Cup (interstate) matches, well-attended test (international) matches and sell-out World Series Cup (one-day international) matches. Local district games are also played there. The cricket season runs from October to March.

Surf Lifesaving Carnivals
The volunteer surf lifesaver is one of Australia's cultural icons, but despite the macho image many surf lifesavers these days are female. You can see lifesavers in action each summer at surf carnivals held all along the coast. Check at a local surf lifesaving club for dates or contact Surf Life Saving NSW (☎ 9984 7188).

Tennis
The Adidas International tennis tournament is held in the 2nd week of January as a prelude to the Australian Open in Melbourne. It's on at the **Olympic Tennis Centre**, Homebush Bay (2, F2). Indoor games are occasionally played at the Sydney Entertainment Centre (☎ 9320 4200) in Haymarket (3, N4).

Yachting

On weekends, hundreds of yachts weave around the ferries and ships on Sydney Harbour. Many are racing, and the most spectacular are the speedy 18-footers. The 18-footer racing season runs from mid-September to late March and the races award big prize money. The oldest and largest 18-footer club is the **Sydney Flying Squadron** (☎ 9955 8350), based at Careening Cove (2 F10) on the northern side of Kirribilli Point.

The greatest yachting event on Sydney Harbour is the Boxing Day (26 December) start of the **Sydney to Hobart Yacht Race**. The harbour is crammed with competitors, media boats and a huge spectator fleet. Special ferries are scheduled by Sydney Ferries to follow the yachts; call ☎ 131500 in November to find out when tickets go on sale.

GAMBLING

Australians love to gamble and Sydney provides plenty of opportunity for punters to be separated from their money. If it runs fast, it's got fans in Sydney – racing, be it of the dog or horse variety, always seems to draw a passionate following.

CASINO
Star City (3, J1)
Star City has all the ambience of a large shopping mall. The gaming rooms, which hold more than 1500 slot machines and 200 betting tables, are decorated in a 'Disney goes Outback' theme. Conventional games like roulette, blackjack and baccarat are supplemented by lesser-known Australian and Asian favourites (two-up, sic bo and pai gow). A variety of restaurants, shops, theatres and bars make up the rest of the complex.
✉ **80 Pyrmont St, Pyrmont (3, J1)**
☎ 9777 9000, 1300 300 711 🚇 Town Hall or Central, then SLR 🚌 443, 888, Star City buses ⛴ Pyrmont wharf ⏲ 24hrs ⑤ free ♿ yes, but not in gaming areas

RACING
Harold Park Raceway
(2, H8) Harness racing every Friday and Tuesday night.
✉ Ross St, Glebe
☎ 9660 3688

Win some or lose some.

Simon Bracken

Royal Randwick
(2, K11) The racetrack closest to the city centre, Royal Randwick is the site for the annual Sydney Cup.
✉ Alison Rd, Randwick
☎ 9663 8400

The Sydney Turf Club
The STC operates the Canterbury Park (☎ 9930 4000) and Rosehill Gardens (☎ 9930 4070) racetracks. The Golden Slipper, run at Rosehill in April, is one of Australia's biggest horse races. Canterbury often has Thursday night racing.
✉ King St, Canterbury (2, K4) & Grand Ave, Rosehill (1, C8)

Wentworth Park
(3, N1) There's greyhound racing at Wentworth Park on Saturday and Monday evenings – the 'Wenty dogs' have been chasing the rabbit here since 1932.
✉ Wattle St, Glebe
☎ 9552 1799

places to stay

There's a huge variety of accommodation in Sydney with good options in every price range.

During the busy summer months, almost every hotel and hostel increases its room rates and cancels any promotional deals it had been offering. Conversely, you can often strike a bargain during the slower winter months. Booking through an accommodation agency, such as the NSW Travel Centre (☎ 132 077), 11-13 York St, can also land you a discount.

Mid-range and top-end hotels publish 'rack' rates (standard rates) but it's worth ringing ahead and asking if any 'special deals' are on offer. Many hotels cater primarily to business people, so they may ask lower rates on weekends. Breakfast and on-site parking is sometimes included in the cost of the room. In Sydney, the view can play a big part in the price of a room.

Room Rates

The price ranges in this chapter indicate the cost per night of a standard double room.

Top End ($$$) from $250
Mid-Range ($$) $100-249
Budget ($) up to $99

If you're looking for budget lodgings, Sydney has plenty of hostels, pubs and guesthouses. Facilities range from basic dorms to well-kept rooms with en-suites (attached bath), TV and share kitchens.

Serviced apartments, which offer hotel-style convenience plus cooking facilities for self-catering, can be good value, especially for families. They vary in size from a hotel room with fridge and microwave to a full-size apartment with three bedrooms.

In the summer holiday season, November to February, prices at beachside resorts can be as much as 40% higher. All inner-city Sydney hotels, serviced apartments and B&Bs are subject to a 10% 'bed tax', which is added to the standard rate. As of July 2000, this tax will be replaced by the GST (also 10%).

Hotels vs Pubs

First-time visitors to Australia may be confused by the distinction between hotels and...well, hotels. There are 3 kinds.

Until relatively recently, any establishment serving alcohol was called a hotel and was legally required to provide accommodation. These hotels are also known as pubs (public houses). Not surprisingly, the accommodation facilities at many were minimal, designed merely to satisfy the licensing authorities. A pub room is usually pretty basic, bathrooms are almost always shared and you probably won't have a phone.

Private hotels are usually boarding-house style places with similar facilities to pubs, but without a bar. These often have the word 'private' in their name to distinguish them from pubs.

Then there are hotels which offer accommodation as well as extra facilities, such as room service etc, and these are usually rated at three stars or higher.

Sydney has a good range of all three types of hotels.

TOP END

ANA Hotel (3, F5)

Luxury ANA-style means suites done up in marble and glass, mist-free mirrors and 'silent minibars' – the harbour views aren't likely to bring you back down to earth either. Of course there's a pool, business centre, multilingual staff, several restaurants and the fantabulous Horizons bar on the 36th floor.

✉ 176 Cumberland St, The Rocks ☎ 9250 6000, 1800 801 080; fax 9250 6250 @ anasales @anahotel.com.au; www.anahotel.com.au 🚇🚌🚢 Circular Quay ✕ cafes, bars, restaurants

Hotel Inter-Continental

(3, F8) Incorporating the beautiful sandstone buildings that once housed the Treasury and the Premier's Office, the Inter-Continental has comfortable, classily appointed rooms. Its environmental mission statement is impressive – food scraps go to the worm farm next door and a comprehensive recycling policy even includes the corks you pop.

✉ 117 Macquarie St, Sydney ☎ 9253 9000, 1800 221 828; fax 9240 1240 @ sydney@ interconti.com; http:// sydney.interconti.com 🚇🚌🚢 Circular Quay ✕ cafes, bars, restaurants

Hotel Nikko (3, K4)

A wavy white facade and stylish rooms make the Nikko the most attractive of the hotels clustering around Darling Harbour. The foyer is built into the original brick and sandstone street frontage, giving it a bit of 'I woz here' cachet.

✉ 161 Sussex St, Darling Harbour ☎ 9299 1231, 1800 222 700; fax 9299 3340 @ reservations@hotel nikko.com.au; www. hotelnikko.com.au 🚇 Town Hall, monorail 🚢 Darling Harbour ✕ bars, restaurants

Manly Pacific Parkroyal (2, B14)

This elegant mid-rise hotel is right on Manly's ocean beach – all rooms have balconies (though they're not all ocean front) and there's a rooftop pool for

days when you'd rather be sand-free.

✉ 55 Nth Steyne, Manly ☎ 9977 7666, 1300 363 300; fax 9977 7822 @ www.parkroyal. com.au 🚢 Manly ✕ bars, restaurants

Observatory Hotel

(3, E4) If it's not the marble bathroom with oversize bath, the mono-grammed robe or the feather doona, it must be the indoor pool with its magical twinkling starry sky that makes the Observatory special. A flotation tank session is complimentary for overseas travellers, though if there's anywhere in Sydney you might not mind giving in to jet lag, it's here.

✉ 89-113 Kent St, Millers Point ☎ 9256 2222, 1800 806 245; fax 9256 2233 @ observatory@mail.com; www.observatory hotel. com.au 🚌 339, 431-4 ✕ bar, restaurant

Old Sydney Parkroyal

(3, D6) The Parkroyal has a great location – check out the views from the rooftop pool if you need convincing. Rooms are better than adequate but the fittings keep the hotel at the bottom end of the top end.

✉ 55 George St, The Rocks ☎ 9252 0524; fax 9251 2093 @ reservations@sphc.com. au; www.sphc.com.au 🚇🚌🚢 Circular Quay ✕ bar, restaurant

Park Hyatt (3, C6)

The Park Hyatt has one of the best locations in Sydney

The Hotel Inter-Continental incorporates historic sandstone buildings in its design.

INTERCONTINENTAL

– on the waterfront at the edge of Campbells Cove, in the shadow of the Harbour Bridge, facing the Opera House. The rooms are elegant and have remote control curtains – what more can we say?

✉ **7 Hickson Rd, Campbells Cove** ☎ **9241 1234, 131234; fax 9256 1555 @** sydney@hyatt.com.au; www.hyatt.com 🚻 🚌 🚊 Circular Quay ✗ bar, restaurant

Post Office Cottage

This charming self-contained sandstone cottage, formerly the Hunters Hill post office, is perfect for those who want to feel like they're not just visiting. It's tastefully furnished with antiques; the dining and garden areas make entertaining a breeze, and the 'spirit bottles are always full'. It's 15mins by taxi from the city or a 20min stroll from the ferry wharf.

✉ **16 Ferry St, Hunters Hill (2, E6)** ☎ **0419 981 648** 🚌 **358** 🚊 from Circular Quay

The Regent (3, F6)

The Regent is all class – excellent views, great location, the largest rooftop pool in town, an attentive concierge and little extras like daily shoe shine. Aaaah.

✉ **199 George St, Sydney** ☎ **9238 0000; fax 9251 2851 @** regent@att.net.au; www.fourseasons.com 🚻 🚌 🚊 Circular Quay ✗ bars, restaurants

Ritz-Carlton (3, F8)

The Ritz-Carlton would scream elegance, if it weren't so inelegant to scream. It's brilliantly located, over the road from the Botanic Gardens. The Victorian building, the courteous, helpful staff, and the lap-of-luxury rooms will have you looking for an excuse to return.

✉ **93 Macquarie St, Sydney** ☎ **9252 4600, 1300 361 180; fax 9252 4759 @** www.ritzcarlton.com 🚻 🚌 🚊 Circular Quay ✗ bar, restaurant

Sheraton on the Park

(3, K7) From the magnificent lobby with maroon marble columns to the fastidious way your bed is turned down each night, the Sheraton is heaven. The location is great for business or pleasure and the facilities make indulgences suddenly seem of absolute necessity.

✉ **161 Elizabeth St, Sydney** ☎ **9286 6000; fax 9286 6686 @** www.sheraton.com 🚻 St James ✗ cafes, bars, restaurants

MID-RANGE

The Hughenden

(4, K9) Victorian Italianate manor-turned-guesthouse with plenty of charm, a mere tickle from Paddington and Centennial Park. The rooms aren't spacious but they're nicely furnished and with such a lovely drawing room and high tea on Sundays, who'd stay shut away?

✉ **14 Queen St, Woollahra** ☎ **9363 4863; fax 9362 0398 @** hughendenhotel@ozemail.com.au 🚌 **378, 380, 382, L82** ✗ cafe, restaurant

The Kirketon (4, D4)

The Kirketon's designer rooms are as impeccably turned out as its clientele.

Stylishly sparse suites are enhanced by ultra-swish niceties like Aveda toiletries, Lindt chocolates and monogrammed bathrobes. The lobby restaurant, *Salt*, is Sydney's newest groovy foodie haunt.

✉ **229 Darlinghurst Rd, Darlinghurst** ☎ **9332 2011; fax 9332 2499 @** info@kirketon.com.au; www.kirketon.com.au 🚌 Kings Cross 🚌 **330, 323-7, 365, 366, L24** ✗ Salt (restaurant), Fix (bar)

Manhattan Park Inn

(4, B6) A friendly hotel better suited to the traveller than the business boffin. The rooms are not flash but are well equipped and some are blessed with harbour views. Art Deco features – tilework, a fancy chrome lift and the cocktail bar – keep the Manhattan out of the doldrums.

✉ **8 Greenknowe Ave, Elizabeth Bay** ☎ **9358 1288; fax 9357 3696 @** manhattan@khll.com 🚌 Kings Cross 🚌 **311** ✗ restaurant

Medusa (4, E4)

Attracting designer-loving darlings, Medusa's shocking pink exterior merely hints at the witty, luscious decor inside. Small, colour-saturated rooms boast enormous beds, mod-con bathrooms and to-die-for furnishings. Ground floor suites open onto a tranquil courtyard and a reflection pool: instant meditative relief from the bustling cafe culture outside.

✉ 267 Darlinghurst Rd, Darlinghurst ☎ 9331 1000; fax 9380 6901 ❻ info@medusa.com.au; www.medusa.com.au. 🚇 Kings Cross 🚌 330, 323-7, 365, 366, L24

Mercure Hotel

This comfortable hotel at Railway Square is a good base for business (desks, email and fax access are standard) and pleasure (Chinatown, city shops and the theatre district are nearby). All rooms have cable TV, city views and the rates include access to the gym and rooftop pool.

✉ 818-20 George St, Sydney (off map) ☎ 9217 6666, 1300 65 65 65; fax 9217 6888 ❻ mercuresydney@big pond.com. 🚇🚌 Central ✕ cafe, restaurant

Ravesi's

A small hotel right across the road from Australia's most famous beach. With its great position, comfortable rooms and

friendly, attentive staff, it feels like it should be a real dollar burner, but it's extremely good value.

✉ cnr Campbell Pde & Hall St, Bondi Beach (2, J13) ☎ 9365 4422; fax 9365 1481 🚌 380 ✕ restaurant

Regent's Court

This Art Deco apartment block has been converted into furnished en-suite rooms with small, impecc-ably stocked kitchens. The rooftop garden is a great place to relax and the staff are well informed.

✉ 18 Springfield Ave, Potts Point (4, C5) ☎ 9358 1533; fax 9358 1833 ❻ regcourt@ iname.com; www.regentscourt.com.au 🚇 Kings Cross 🚌 330, 323-7, 365, 366, 387, L24

Rockfort

With the Harbour Bridge down the road, Walsh Bay out back and The Rocks all around, Rockfort could ride on location alone. What a bonus that it's also one of the city's most charming, boutique B&Bs, filled with art and antiques.

✉ 61 Lower Fort St, The Rocks (3, D5) ☎

9251 9475; fax 9251 9552 ❻ www.rockfort. citysearch.com.au 🚌 433 ✕ breakfast available

Russell Hotel

Its traditionally decorated rooms, pleasant lounge areas and roof garden make the Russell a choice getaway from The Rocks' bustle. Though some rooms are small and none have TVs, they've all got character and – lovely! – fresh flowers.

✉ 143a George St, The Rocks (3, E6) ☎ 9241 3543; fax 9252 1652 ❻ russhtl@zip.com.au 🚇 🚌 🚆 Circular Quay ✕ restaurant

Simpsons of Potts Point (4, A5)

This superb heritage home has been faithfully restored and converted into a quiet, tasteful B&B. The rooms are spacious, have en-suites (the Cloud Suite has a private spa) and there's a lounge with a piano if you want to mingle or tinkle.

✉ 8 Challis Ave, Potts Point ☎ 9356 2199; fax 9356 4476 ❻ www.simpsonspottspoint. com.au 🚇 Kings Cross 🚌 from airport

Tasteful Victorian-era comforts at Tricketts B&B

Simon Bracken

Tricketts Bed & Breakfast

Give thanks that such a gorgeous Victorian home is open to guests – it's a treat. The rooms are large and tastefully decked out; some have glass bricked bathrooms. The kitchen and living areas are large,

there's a snooker table, and the atmosphere is friendly.
✉ 270 Glebe Pt Rd, Glebe (2, H3) ☎ 9552 1141; fax 9692 9462 🚌 431-34

Victoria Court Hotel

(4, B5) This comfortable boutique hotel occupies 2

restored terrace houses. The staff are friendly and the rooms lovely. Security parking is an added bonus.
✉ 122 Victoria St, Potts Point ☎ 9357 3200; fax 9357 7606 🅮 info@ victoriacourt.com.au; www.victoriacourt.com. au 🚃 Kings Cross

BUDGET

Alishan International Guesthouse

Both a guesthouse and an upmarket hostel, the Alishan boasts well-travelled, multilingual staff. There are good common areas, including kitchen, laundry and a small garden with barbecue. Computer facilities are available.
✉ 100 Glebe Point Rd, Glebe (2, H8) ☎ 9566 4048; fax 9525 4686 🅮 kevin@alishan.com.au; www.alishan.com.au 🚌 431-4

Australian Sunrise Lodge

Clean, pleasant, secure and well-managed, the Sunrise is a real bargain. The rooms are bright and have tea and coffee facilities, fridges and TV, but no phone. There are fully equipped kitchens and complimentary lock-up parking nearby.
✉ 485 King St, Newtown (2, J8) ☎ 9550 4999; fax 9550 4457 🚃 Newtown 🚌 422, 423, 426, 428

Billabong Gardens

A good hostel, purpose-built by one of Sydney's original hostel owners. It's bustling but clean, full of backpackers splashing in the small pool. Undercover parking is available.

✉ 5-11 Egan St, Newtown (2, J8) ☎ 9550 3236; fax 9550 4352 🅮 book@billabonggardens .com.au 🚃 Newtown 🚌 422, 423, 426, 428

CB Private Hotel

(3, N6) First opened for business in 1908, this was once the largest residential hotel in the country. It's still going strong. There are over 200 rooms, mostly singles, all with shared bathroom, and reasonably well maintained.
✉ 417 Pitt St, Sydney ☎ 9211 5115; fax 9281 9605 🚃 Central, monorail

Palisade Hotel (3, D4)

Pub rooms mean you share a bathroom and you don't get a phone, but when the sheets are clean, and harbour and river views are under a hundred bucks,

who cares? The Palisade is low key and local in a killer location – get in before it's renovated!
✉ 35 Bettington St, Millers Point ☎ 9247 2272; fax 9247 2040 🚌 431-34 ✕ lunch Mon-Fri, dinner Mon-Sat

Sydney Central YHA

(3, P5) Spotless twin rooms with bathroom, right in the centre of Sydney for under $70? Crazy but true! This massive hostel is well run and has a heated rooftop pool and a licensed cafe. There's a travel agency on-site.
✉ cnr Pitt St & Rawson Pl ☎ 9281 9111; fax 9281 9199 🅮 syd central@yhansw.org .au; www.yha.org.au 🚃 🚌 Central ✕ cafe (fully licensed)

Great location and good value – Sydney Central YHA

Tremayne Private Hotel

This large guesthouse may induce boarding school flashbacks – it's a bit of a warren and the mood is not particularly friendly. That said, the rooms are pretty good, things are kept clean and the suburb is a quiet base from which to explore Sydney.

✉ 89 Carabella St, Kirribilli (2, F10) ☎ 9955 4155 🅿 🚇 Milsons Point 🚌 269 ✕ no

YWCA (3, N7)

The rooms – ranging from dorms to doubles – are simple but spotless and well-furnished. The position is enviable: Hyde Park is across the road, and the city centre and Oxford St are a short walk away. Both men and women can stay here.

✉ 5-11 Wentworth Ave, Sydney ☎ 9264 2451, 1800 249 124; fax 9285 6288 @ y-hotel@zip.com.au 🚇 Museum ✕ cafe

SERVICED APARTMENTS

2 Bond St $$$

If you're taking care of business, 2 Bond St will take care of you. There are modem connections and two direct-dial phones in each room and 24hr room service for those number-crunching all-nighters. There are women only floors; cots and high chairs are available free.

✉ 2 Bond St, Sydney (3, G6) ☎ 9250 9555, 1800 222 226; fax 9250 9556 @ www.2bondst.com.au 🚌 any along George St ✕ cafe

Carrington Sydney City Centre Apartments $$

Self-contained city centre apartments with no views and no frills. Reception is on the 10th floor.

✉ 57-9 York St, Sydney (3, H5) ☎ 9299 6556; fax 9299 2727 🚇 Wynyard 🚌 171, 188, 190

Manly Paradise $$

Set right on Manly ocean beach, the apartments are comfortable without being luxurious, sleep 5 and have balconies overlooking the beach. There's a rooftop pool and motel rooms are also available.

✉ 54 Nth Steyne, Manly (2, B14) ☎ 9977 5799, 1800 815 789; fax 9977 6848 @ enquiries@manlyparadise.com.au; www.manlyparadise.com.au 🚢 Manly

Parkridge City Apartments $$

If you're staying in Sydney for a couple of weeks, Parkridge is a good place to set up. The apartments are spacious and liveable, though not deluxe. There is a pool, spa, sauna and free undercover parking in the building.

✉ 6-14 Oxford St, Sydney (3, N8) ☎ 9361 8600; fax 9361 8666 @ parkridge@hotel-apartments.com.au; www.hotel-apartments.com.au 🚇 Museum 🚌 380, 382

Quay West $$

Jostling the heavyweight hotels in this part of town, Quay West offers no-fuss quality apartments. It's a good alternative for the business traveller who wants to be close to the action, but doesn't need chocolates left on the pillow every afternoon.

✉ 98 Gloucester St, The Rocks (3, F5) ☎ 9240 6000, 1800 805 031; fax 9240 6060 @ resqws@mirvachotels.com.au 🚇🚌🚢 Circular Quay ✕ restaurant

York Apartment Hotel $$

Rates for these spacious flats with balconies include parking. From the 6th-floor swimming pool, you can see the approaches to Sydney Harbour Bridge.

✉ 5 York St, Sydney (3, G5) ☎ 9210 5000; fax 9290 1487 @ york@acay.com.au; www.theyorkapartments.com.au 🚇 Wynyard 🚌 202, 263 ✕ restaurant

Balmain Lodge $

These simply furnished studio apartments are good value, especially if you're staying long enough to take advantage of generous weekly rates. Each apartment sleeps 2, has TV, microwave, fridge and tea and coffee making facilities; bathrooms are shared between two units.

✉ 415 Darling St, Balmain (2, F8) ☎ 9810 3700; fax 9810 1500 🚌 433, 441, 442, 445, 446 ✕ restaurant

facts for the visitor

Ben Hawkins

PRE-DEPARTURE
Travel Requirements

Passport
Must be valid for 6 months from date of entry.

Visa
Required for all visitors except New Zealand nationals. Visa applications are available from Australian diplomatic missions or travel agents.

Return/Onward Ticket
Not compulsory, but immigration officials may question your entry intentions if you don't have one.

Immunisations
Required only if you've visited an infected country in the preceding 14 days.

Travel Insurance
A policy that covers theft, loss, flight cancellations and medical problems is a must; check with your travel agent.

Driving Permit
Visitors can drive using their home-country driving licence.

Keeping Copies
Photocopy important documents (keep them separate from the originals) and leave a copy at home. You can also store details of documents in Lonely Planet's free online Travel Vault, password-protected and accessible world-wide. Log on to www.ekno.lonely planet.com for details.

Tourist Information Abroad

The Australian Tourist Commission (ATC) conducts most of its customer relations through its efficient Web site, www.australia.com. The ATC also maintains telephone 'help-lines' in the USA (☎ 661-775 2000), UK (☎ 171 940 5200) and New Zealand (☎ 64-9527 1629).

Tourism NSW has a similar, but smaller Web site (www.tourism. nsw.gov.au/tnsw/index_contents/ index.html). Both bodies operate travel trade offices, including:

Japan
  ATC: Australian Business Centre, New Otani Garden Court Bldg, 28F, 4-1, Kioi-cho, Chiyoda-Ku, Tokyo, 102 (☎ 3-5214 0720; fax 5214 0719)

  Tourism NSW: address as above (☎ 3-5214 0777; fax 5214 0780)

New Zealand
  ATC: L13, 44-48 Emily Pl, Auckland 1 (☎ 09-379 9594; fax 307 3117)

  Tourism NSW: address as above (☎ 09-379 9118; fax 366 6173)

UK
  ATC: Gemini House, 10-18 Putney Hill, London SW15 6AA (☎ 020-8780 2229; fax 8780 1496)

  Tourism NSW: L2, Australia Centre, The Strand, London WC2B4LC (☎ 020-7887 5003; fax 7836 5266)

USA
  ATC: 2049 Century Park East, Suite 1920, Los Angeles, CA, 90067 (☎ 310-229 4870; fax 552 1215)

  Tourism NSW: 13737 Fiji Way, Suite C10, Marina Del Rey, CA 90292 (☎ 310-301 1903; fax 301 0913)

Climate & When to Go

Sydney is comfortable to visit at any time of the year, but unless you enjoy lots of sun keep away in summer.

Autumn is delightful especially around March-April, with clear warm days and mild nights. In spring (Sept-Nov) there's more chance of rain, but it usually clears

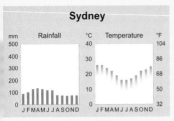

Sydney
Rainfall | Temperature

quickly. Average summer temperatures are around 25°C (77°F), though it can get up to 40°C (104°F) on a hot day. Humidity is high but torrential downpours often break the heat from October to March.

January is the peak of the school-holiday season. Other school holidays fall around March-April (Easter), late June to mid-July, and late September to early October.

ARRIVAL & DEPARTURE

Sydney can be reached by direct flights from the UK, Europe, Japan, North America and New Zealand. Airfares to Australia are expensive, but advance-purchase fares and other special deals can reduce ticket prices considerably. Generally, the Australian summer (Dec-Feb) is the most expensive time to fly into the country, and May and September the cheapest. Within Australia, Sydney is accessible by air, train, bus and road, and it's a popular port for cruise ships.

Air

Kingsford Smith (1, C9), 10km south of the city centre, is Sydney's major airport. The international and domestic terminals are a 4km ($2.50) bus trip apart. Ansett and Qantas have separate but adjoining domestic terminals.

Left-Luggage
Large lockers are available in the domestic and international arrivals halls. Oversize items can only be stored in the international lockers.

Information
General Inquiries
☎ 9667 9111

Flight Information
| Qantas | ☎ 131 223 |
| Ansett | ☎ 131 515 |

Carpark Information
| International | ☎ 9669 3693 |
| Domestic/long-term | ☎ 9667 4382 |

Airport Access
Bus Kingsford Smith Transport/ Airporter (☎ 9667 0663/3800) runs a 24hr service between the airport and central Sydney hotels.

The Airport Express (☎ 131 500) serves major Sydney suburbs, including Bondi ($6.50/4 one-way; $11/5.50 return).

Manly Airport Bus (☎ 9955 0192) costs around $18 (bookings essential).

Taxi To Circular Quay $20-25; to Central Station $15-20.

Train A rail link to Central station is due to open in May 2000.

Bus

Interstate and regional bus travellers arrive at Sydney coach terminal (☎ 9281 9366), on Eddy Ave (3, P5) outside Central station. It's open 6am-10.30pm daily. All major bus companies have offices nearby.

Train

Sydney's main rail terminus for interstate and principal regional services is Central station (3, P6), also known as Sydney Terminal station.

For information, train arrival and departure times and bookings, call ☎ 132232. Tickets can be bought from the station ticket office from 6am-9.35pm.

Customs

All goods of animal or vegetable origin must be declared, as authorities are keen to prevent weeds, pests or diseases getting into the country. When you leave, don't take protected flora or fauna with you. Amounts of more than $A10,000 in banknotes or coins must be reported on arrival.

At Sydney airport there are 2 colour-coded customs channels: green (nothing to declare) and red (something to declare).

Duty Free

Travellers over 18 may import 1L of alcoholic liquor and 250 cigarettes or 250g of tobacco products.

Duty/tax-free allowances of $A400 per person aged 18 or over and $A200 per person under 18 are granted for other goods intended as gifts.

Departure Tax

Departure tax is prepaid – it is included in the price of your ticket.

GETTING AROUND

Trains, buses and ferries are generally convenient, reliable and good value. Be aware that if you're caught without a ticket, you're liable for a $100 on-the-spot fine.

Call the State Transit Authority (STA) of NSW (☎ 131500) for information about Sydney buses, ferries and CityRail, or visit their Circular Quay information booths or Web site (www.sta.nsw.gov. au).

The Public Transport Authority (PTA) has an excellent Web site (www.sydneytransport.net.au) with links to the STA, Countrylink and the private bus companies.

Travel Passes

The SydneyPass ($85/115/135 for 3/5/7 days) offers bus, rail and ferry transport, travel on the Sydney Explorer and Bondi & Bay Explorer buses, harbour ferry cruises and a return trip on the Airport Express.

Train

CityRail

Sydney's suburban rail network is the fastest mode of public transport around town. Trains run from around 4am-midnight. There are automatic ticket machines at most stations but humans are usually on hand too. An information booth at Circular Quay, behind Wharf 5, is open 9am-5pm daily. For information call ☎ 131500.

Monorail

The monorail circles Darling Harbour and links it to the city centre. There's a train every 4mins, and the full circuit takes 14mins ($3; day pass $6). For information call ☎ 9552 2288.

Sydney Light Rail

The SLR runs 24hrs between Central station and Wentworth Park via Chinatown, Darling Harbour and Pyrmont ($3-4; day pass $6). For information call ☎ 9660 5288.

Bus

Buses run almost everywhere, but they're slow compared to trains. Bondi Beach, Coogee and parts of the North Shore are only serviced by buses. Nightrider buses provide a skeleton service after the regular buses and trains stop running around midnight.

Sydney is divided into 7 zones, the city centre being 'zone 1'. The main bus stops in the city centre are Circular Quay (3, F7), Wynyard Park on York St (3, H5) and Railway Square (3, P5).

You can buy tickets from newsagents, kiosks, and on the bus (correct change appreciated). Fares start at $1.30; most trips will be $2.50 or less.

The information kiosk on the corner of Alfred and Pitt Sts (3, F6) is open 8am-8pm. There are other kiosks near Wynyard station on Carrington St (3, H5) and outside the Queen Victoria Building (3, K5) on York St.

Special Services

Sydney Explorer A red STA bus that does a 2hr, 22-stop circular route from Circular Quay through Kings Cross, Chinatown, Darling Harbour and The Rocks. It runs about every 20mins from 8.40am-5.25pm daily. Tickets are $28/20 and can be bought on the bus.

Bondi & Bay Explorer A blue bus that does 2hr loops of the inner city and eastern suburbs, including Paddington, Double Bay, Vaucluse, Watsons Bay and Bondi beach. Departs from Circular Quay (3, F7)

every half-hour from 9.15am-4.15pm daily. Tickets are $28/20.

Useful Routes from Circular Quay

Balmain	441, 442, 445, 446
Bondi Beach	380, 382, 389
Coogee	314-16, 372-4, 377, X13, X74
Darling Harbour	443, 456, 500, 506, 888
Glebe	431-4
Kings Cross	200, 323-7, 333
La Perouse	393-4, 398
Leichhardt	370, 413, 436-40, 445, 446
Newtown	355, 370, 422-3, 426, 428
Paddington	378, 380, 382
Surry Hills	301-04, 375, 390, 391
Watsons Bay	324, 325

Taxi

Taxis are available for hire when the light on top is lit up. They are easily flagged down in the city centre and inner suburbs. On Friday and Saturday nights, there are patrolled taxi ranks at the Regent Hotel (3, F6), on Phillip St opposite the Wentworth Hotel (3, H7) and on Park St between George & Pitt Sts (3, L6). You'll also often find cabs in taxi ranks at Central, Wynyard and Circular Quay train stations.

The 4 big taxi companies offer a reliable telephone service: try Taxis Combined (☎ 8332 8888); RSL Taxis (☎ 132211); Legion (☎ 131451); or Premier Radio Cabs (☎ 131017).

Fares & Charges

Flagfall is $2.20, then it's $1.22/km. If you want the cabbie to wait, it's 58c a minute, and there's a charge of 10c/kg for luggage over 25kg (often waived). Booking costs $1 extra.

Approximate Fares

Within City Centre	$8
City–Newtown	$10
City–Bondi Beach	$25
City–Airport	$25

Ferry

All the harbour ferries, JetCats and RiverCats depart from Circular Quay. The STA, which runs most ferries, has an information and ticket office on the concourse opposite the entry to Wharf 4. Fares are usually $3.20-5; many ferries have connecting bus services.

Hegarty's Ferries (☎ 9206 1167) run from Wharf 6 to Lavender Bay, McMahons Point and Kirribilli, directly across the harbour.

Water Taxi

Water Taxis (☎ 9955 3222) and Harbour Taxis (☎ 9555 1155) can be chartered from Circular Quay to Watsons Bay ($40 for one person, $5 for each extra person), Clarke Island ($25/5) and Shark Island ($35/5). All fares are one-way; pick-ups can be arranged.

Car & Motorcycle

Avoid bringing a car into Sydney. The city centre has an extensive, confusing one-way street system; parking is hell; and tow-away zones are common. Private car parks are expensive – city centre prices are around $7/hr.

On the other hand, if you want to tour around, a car is great. Many hotels include parking in accommodation packages. Red light and speed cameras are common and car rental companies will send you any fines you incur, usually with a hefty 'processing fee' added.

Road Rules

Vehicles drive on the left-hand side of the road, seat belts are compulsory (both front and back seat) and motorcyclists must wear helmets. Minimum driving age is 18.

Speed Limits The limit is 60km/h in built-up areas and 100-110km/h on freeways.

Drink-Driving The blood-alcohol limit of 0.05% is enforced with random breath checks and severe punishments.

Car Rental

The major companies – Avis (☎ 9353 9000), Budget (☎ 132727) and Hertz (☎ 133039, 1800 550 067 international) – all have offices at the airport and in the city. Thrifty is a smaller, national company with desks at the airport (☎ 9669 6677) and offices around the city. Expect to pay around $60 a day for a compact car. Unleaded petrol costs around 75c a litre.

Motoring Organisations

The National Roads & Motorists Association, or NRMA (☎ 132132; 151 Clarence St), provides 24hr emergency roadside assistance (☎ 131111), travel advice, insurance and discounted accommodation. It has reciprocal arrangements with similar organisations overseas.

PRACTICAL INFORMATION

Tourist Information

There's a tourist information booth near Wharf 6, Circular Quay (3, F7) and a Sydney Information Booth in Martin Place (3, J7). Also try:

NSW Travel Centre
(☎ 132077) Provides statewide accommodation and travel advice. Its Sydney airport counter (☎ 9667 6050), in the

international arrivals hall, is open 6.30am-midnight.

Sydney Visitors Centre

(☎ 9255 1788, 1800 067 676) 106 George St, The Rocks (3, D6). Also serves as an accommodation agency.

Countrylink Travel Centres

(☎ 132232) They do special deals on accommodation; there are several offices around town, including 11-13 York St (3, H5) and at Central station (3, P6).

Travellers' Information Service

(☎ 9281 9366) At Central station coach terminal, this is a super helpful, if busy, place for assistance with accommodation, bookings, luggage lockers, coach tickets, local transport information and maps. It's open 6am-10.30pm daily.

Tourist Information Service

(☎ 9669 5111) Answers phone inquiries from 8am-6pm.

Consulates

Most foreign embassies are based in Canberra, but many countries have a consulate in central Sydney, including:

Japan

(☎ 9231 3455) 52 Martin Pl (3, J7)

New Zealand

(☎ 9247 1344) 1 Alfred Sq, Circular Quay (3, F6)

UK

(☎ 9247 7521) 1 Macquarie Pl (3, F7)

USA

(☎ 9373 9200) 19-29 Martin Pl (3, H6)

Money

Currency

The unit of currency is the Australian dollar, which is divided into 100 cents. When paying cash, prices are rounded up or down to the nearest 5 cents.

There are coins for $2, $1, 50c, 20c, 10c, and 5c, and notes for $100, $50, $20, $10, and $5.

Travellers Cheques

Accepted in banks, larger hotels and duty free stores. American Express (☎ 9271 1111) and Thomas Cook (☎ 9229 6611) are widely recognised; they don't charge for cashing their own cheques and can usually arrange replacement cheques on the spot if you lose yours. Australian dollar travellers cheques can be exchanged at banks without incurring commissions or fees.

Credit Cards

Visa, MasterCard, Diners Club and American Express are widely accepted. For lost cards contact:

American Express	☎ 9271 8666
Diners Club	☎ 1300 360 060
MasterCard	☎ 1800 120 113 (Australian cardholders contact issuing bank)
Visa	☎ 1800 805 341

Changing Money

Foreign exchange branches may offer marginally better exchange rates than banks, and usually have longer opening hours and queue-free service. Always check the rates, commissions and any other charges. For foreign exchange rates, call ☎ 1900 951 125.

Tipping

Cloakroom attendants	no
Guides	no
Hairdressers	no
Porters	$2-5
Restaurants	10%
Room cleaners	no
Taxis	round up to $
Theatre ushers	no

Taxes

GST

From July 2000, the Australian Government will introduce a 10% goods and services tax, or GST. This tax will be automatically added to almost anything you buy, though some basic food items will be exempt.

Discounts

Student/Youth Cards

Most tourist attractions recognise ISIC card-holders. However, international student cards aren't valid for concession fares on local transport.

Senior Citizens

Some places may agree to give you a discount if you show your seniors card from home though most seniors discounts are restricted to Australians.

Opening Hours

Banks
Mon-Thurs 9.30am-4pm, Fri 9.30am-5pm. Some large city branches open Mon-Thurs 8am-6pm, and Fridays until 9pm.

Post Offices
9am-5pm; some open Sat 10am-2pm.

Shops
Most are open Mon-Wed & Fri 9am-5.30pm, Thurs 9am-9pm, Sat 9am-5pm and Sun 11am-4pm.

Pharmacies
Most 8am-6pm, some later (p. 117).

Tourist Sites
9am-5pm (some are closed Mon)

Public Holidays

New Year's Day	1 Jan
Australia Day	26 Jan
Good Friday	Mar/Apr
Easter Monday	Mar/Apr
Anzac Day	25 Apr
Queen's Birthday	June (2nd Mon)
August Bank Holiday	Aug (1st Mon)
Labour Day	Oct (1st Mon)
Christmas Day	25 Dec
Boxing Day	26 Dec

Banks, businesses and stores are closed on public holidays. Museums and other attractions might close on Christmas Day and Boxing Day.

Time

Sydney is on Eastern Standard Time, which is 10hrs ahead of GMT/UTC. Eastern Summer time is 1hr ahead of standard time (last Sunday in October to last Sunday in March).

At noon in Sydney it's:
2am in London
4am in Cape Town
11am in Tokyo
2pm in Auckland
6pm the previous day in Los Angeles
9pm the previous day in New York

Electricity

Standard voltage throughout Australia is 220-240 volts AC, 50Hz.

Plugs are flat 3-pin. Bring converters for US flat 2-pin plugs or European round 2-pin plugs used with electric shavers or hair driers from home as they're difficult to find. Adaptors for British plugs are found in good hardware shops, chemists and travel agents.

Weights & Measures

Australia uses the metric system, though in country areas you may still hear people talking in imperial units – check when asking directions. See the conversion table on page 121.

Post

Australia Post (☎ 131318) runs the country's mail system.

Sydney's general post office, or GPO (3, J6), is in the grand Victorian building on Martin Place. A GPO counter service (☎ 9244 3700) is around the corner on 130 Pitt St.

Sending Mail

Stamps are sold at post office counters, Australia Post retail outlets, and post offices operating from newsagencies.

Opening Hours

Post offices open Mon-Fri 9am-5pm. Larger ones, such as the GPO, also open Sat 10am-2pm.

Telephone

Public payphones are either coin or card-operated; local calls cost 40c. Some also accept credit cards.

Phonecards

Local and international phonecards range in value from $5-50 and are available from retail outlets which display the phonecard logo.

Lonely Planet's eKno Communication Card, specifically aimed at travellers, provides competitive international calls (avoid using it for local calls), messaging services and free email.

For information on joining and accessing the service, log on to www.ekno.lonelyplanet.com.

Useful Numbers

Directory Inquiries	☎	013
Int'l Directory Inquiries	☎	1225
Operator	☎	1234
Int'l Dialling Code	☎	0011
Interpreters	☎	131450
Reverse Charge Calls	☎	12550

Recorded Information

News	☎	1900 954 954
Time	☎	1194
Weather	☎	1196

International Codes

Canada	☎	1
Japan	☎	81
New Zealand	☎	64
South Africa	☎	27
UK	☎	44
USA	☎	1

Home Country Direct

Canada
Bell ☎ 1800 881150
AT&T ☎ 1800 881155

Ireland
☎ 1800 881353

New Zealand
☎ 1800 881640

UK
BT ☎ 1800 881440/1
Mercury ☎ 1800 881417

USA
Bell ☎ 1800 881149
Sprint ☎ 1800 811877

Email/www

You can log on to the Net at most public libraries or at Internet cafes (p. 116). Coin-operated computer stations are also springing up around town. If you want to send or receive email, local service providers can allow you access to your existing POP email account and to other Internet services.

The local access number for CompuServe is ☎ 9465 9600; for AOL call ☎ 8437 8000.

Australia On Line
☎ 1800 621258; www.ozonline.com.au

Telstra Big Pond
☎ 1800 804282; www.bigpond.com

OzEmail
☎ 132884; www.ozemail.com.au

Useful Sites

Start at Lonely Planet's Web site (www.lonelyplanet.com) to get background information on Sydney, travel news, tips from other travellers and links to useful travel resources. Also try:

Australian Tourist Commission
www.australia.com

Commonwealth Bureau of Meteorology
www.BoM.gov.au

State Library of NSW
www.slnsw.gov.au/sydney/sydney.htm

State Transit Authority (STA)
www.sydneytransport.net.au

Sydney City Council
www.sydneycity.nsw.gov.au

Sydney Morning Herald's city guide
www.citysearch.com

Sydney Sidewalk
www.sydney.sidewalk.com.au

Internet Cafes

Global Gossip
(☎ 9326 9777; 111 Darlinghurst Rd, Kings Cross (4, C4); 8am-1am, 20c/min); has lots of modems, phone booths, scanners and mailboxes.

Roobar
(☎ 9361 5846; 253 Crown St, Darlinghurst (4, F2); 8am-6pm, $3/hr); has 5 computers, printers, phone lines and scanners. Meals range from French toast to focaccias.

Well Connected Cafe
(☎ 9566 2655; 35 Glebe Point Rd, Glebe (2, H9); 7.30am-midnight, $6/hr); old terrace house with brightly painted walls, it offers 10 computers scattered over 3 floors. Bagels, cakes and salads are available.

Doing Business

The *Australian Financial Review* and *Business Review Weekly (BRW)* are the foremost publications on business and finance.

Many hotels provide business facilities, including conference rooms, secretarial services, fax and photocopying services, use of computers, private office space and translation services.

At Kingsford Smith airport, the Qantas business lounge offers business travellers a range of services, including individual workstations equipped with telephone, fax, modem point and photocopier.

Newspapers & Magazines

Daily newspapers are the tabloid *Daily Telegraph* and the broadsheets *Sydney Morning Herald*, *The Australian* and *The Australian Financial Review*.

Magazines worth checking out include the *Bulletin* and *HQ*.

Free street papers include *Drum Media*, *Revolver*, *Sydney City Hub* and *Capital Q Weekly*.

Radio & TV

Radio

ABC Radio National
(576 AM) – news & views

2BL
(702 AM) – news & current affairs

ABC Fine Music
(92.9 FM) – classical music

Triple J
(105.7 FM) – youth-oriented music & news

2EA
(1386 AM) – SBS's multilingual station

TV

Sydney has 5 free-to-air channels: Channel 2, the government-funded ABC station; channels 7, 9 and 10, for standard commercial fare; and UHF28, the SBS multicultural broadcaster.

Cable TV is provided by Foxtel and OptusVision.

Photography & Video

Print and slide film is widely available. Film is susceptible to heat, so protect your film by keeping it cool and having it processed as soon as possible. The best photographs are taken early in the morning or late in the afternoon, especially in summer when the sun's glare tends to wash out colours.

Australia uses the Phase Alternative Line (PAL) system which isn't compatible with other video standards unless converted.

Most tourist attractions are pretty relaxed about people snapping photos and filming. The interior of the Opera House theatres are usually subject to copyright and any photography and filming is prohibited. You can't carry a camera on the Harbour Bridge climb.

Health

Precautions
Australia has the world's highest incidence of skin cancer, so cover up and wear plenty of sunscreen. The sun is at its fiercest between 11am and 3pm.

Dehydration or salt deficiency can cause heat exhaustion. Take time to acclimatise to high temperatures and make sure you drink sufficient liquids.

Tap water is drinkable, but many Sydney residents drink bottled water or use water filters.

Insurance & Medical Treatment
Visitors from Finland, Italy, Malta, the Netherlands, New Zealand, Sweden and the UK have reciprocal health rights and can register at any Medicare office (☎ 132011). Travel insurance is advisable to cover other expenses (eg ambulance and repatriation).

Medical Services
Hospitals with 24hr casualty and outpatient departments include:

Royal North Shore Hospital
(☎ 9926 7111) Pacific Highway, St Leonards (2, J7)

Royal Prince Alfred Hospital
(☎ 9515 6111) Missenden Rd, Camperdown (2, H3)

St Vincent's Hospital
(☎ 9339 1111) cnr Victoria & Burton Sts, Darlinghurst (4, F4)

Sydney Children's Hospital
(☎ 9382 1111) High St, Randwick (2, L1)

Sydney Hospital & Sydney Eye Hospital
(☎ 9382 7111) Macquarie St, Sydney (3, J8)

Dental Emergencies
To be referred to your closest dentist call ☎ 9906 1660 from 9am-5pm, and ☎ 9369 7050 from 7pm-8am.

Pharmacies & Drugs
Some chemists with longer opening hours are:

Blake's Pharmacy
(☎ 9358 6712) 28 Darlinghurst Rd, Kings Cross (4, C5); 8am-midnight

Darlinghurst Prescription Pharmacy
(☎ 9361 5882) 261 Oxford St, Darlinghurst (4, F3); 8am-10pm

Park Pharmacy
(☎ 9552 3372) 321 Glebe Point Rd, Glebe (2, H3); 8am-8pm

Wu's Pharmacy
(☎ 9211 1805) 629 George St, Sydney (3, O5); 9am-9pm Mon-Sat, 9am-7pm Sun

Emergency Prescription Service
(☎ 9235 0333) 5pm-9am

HIV/AIDS
Condoms are available from chemists, convenience stores, supermarkets and vending machines in airports and some entertainment venues.

For advice on HIV/AIDS call the AIDS Information Line (☎ 9332 4000) or contact the AIDS Council of NSW (☎ 9206 2000, 1800 063060), PO Box 350, Darlinghurst, NSW 2010.

Emergency Numbers

Ambulance	☎	000
Police	☎	000
Fire Brigade	☎	000
Lifeline	☎	131114
Crisis Centre	☎	9358 6577
Rape Crisis Centre	☎	9819 6565

Toilets

Clean, free, accessible toilets are common in Sydney. It's very unusual to be asked to pay. Toilets are generally unattended and reasonably clean and safe. Disabled access is usually provided in newer buildings but may be a struggle in older places.

Safety Concerns

Sydney isn't a dangerous city but the usual big-city rules apply:

- Never leave cars or rooms unlocked
- Never leave luggage unattended
- Never show big wads of money
- Never get drunk in the company of strangers
- Be extra cautious in touristy or red light areas (eg Kings Cross)
- Report any crimes to the nearest police station

Beach Safety

Don't go swimming if you've been drinking alcohol. Swimming after a heavy meal is also unwise. If you get into trouble when you're in the water, raise your arm and keep it raised while treading water or floating until help arrives.

Shark attacks are extremely rare, but if a siren sounds while you're swimming leave the water quickly but calmly.

There are a few poisonous marine animals (such as the blue-ringed octopus, which can be fatal) – so if you don't know what it is, don't touch it.

Some beaches are unsuitable for swimming because of pollution caused by stormwater runoff; radio stations and newspapers give updates on the latest conditions.

Lost Property

If you've lost something on public transport, call ☎ 9379 4757 from 8.30am-4pm Monday to Friday.

Women Travellers

Sydney is generally safe for women travellers, although you should avoid walking alone late at night. Sexual harassment and discrimination, while uncommon, can occur and shouldn't be tolerated. However, instead of reacting strongly to infantile sexism from drunken louts in pubs or bars, it's better to leave and choose a better place – there are plenty.

The contraceptive pill is available on prescription only, so a visit to the doctor is necessary. Tampons are available from chemists and supermarkets. Many hotels have rooms, sometimes even whole floors, reserved for women.

Organisations

Some of the major women's organisations are:

Royal Hospital for Women
(☎ 9382 6111) Barker St, Randwick (2, L1)

Women & Girls Emergency Centre
(☎ 9360 5388) 177 Albion St, Surry Hills (4, H2)

Women's Legal Resources Centre
(☎ 9749 5533, 1800 801 501)

Women's Liberation House
(☎ 9569 3819) 63 Palace St, Petersham (2, F2)

Gay & Lesbian Travellers

Gay and lesbian culture is so strong

in Sydney that it's almost main-stream. Oxford St, especially around Taylor Square (4, F2), is the centre of what is probably the second-largest gay community in the world.

The suburb of Newtown is home to the city's lesbian scene. Sydney is one of the top holiday destinations for North American gays and lesbians.

Despite this, there's still a strong homophobic streak amongst some sections of the community, and violence against homosexuals isn't unknown.

In NSW, it's legal for a man to have sex with a man over the age of 18, and for a woman to have sex with a woman over the age of 16.

Information & Organisations
Two free gay papers, *Capital Q Weekly* and *Sydney Star Observer*, and publications such as *Lesbians on the Loose (LOTL)* have extensive listings.

For counselling and referral call the Gay & Lesbian Line (☎ 9207 2800), daily from 4pm-midnight.

Senior Travellers

For information on recreational and other activities contact the Seniors Information Service (☎ 131 244), 6th fl, 93 York St (3, K5).

Each March, there's a Seniors Week with exhibitions, concerts and seminars.

Disabled Travellers

Wheelchair Access
Most of Sydney's attractions are accessible to wheelchair travellers. All new or renovated places cater for wheelchair access with ramps, toilets and special facilities. Older buildings are harder to access with wheelchairs, though most of the National Trust's Historic Houses are

at least partially accessible. Attendants can usually show you photos of inaccessible areas.

A number of taxis accommodate wheelchairs – advise the operator when making a booking.

Hearing Loops
Most of Sydney's major attractions offer hearing loops and sign language interpreters for hearing impaired travellers. In all cases, it's advisable to make your needs known in advance.

Parking
Sydney has lots of parking spaces reserved for disabled drivers. Disabled travellers coming from overseas should contact the Roads and Traffic Authority to obtain a temporary parking permit (☎ 9218 6888, 1800 624384; fax 9843 3850).

Information & Organisations
The City of Sydney Web site lists toilets, restaurants, parking and telephones with wheelchair access at: www.cityofsydney.nsw.gov.au/cs_disabled_services.asp. Also check the following:

NICAN
(☎ 6285 3713, 1800 806769; fax 6285 3714) Box 407 Curtin, 2605 ACT; provides information on accommodation and recreation

Deaf Society of NSW
(☎ 9893 8555/8858) L4, 169 Macquarie St, Parramatta, 2150 (1, C8)

Royal Blind Society of NSW
(☎ 9334 3333) 4 Mitchell St, Enfield, 2136 (2, G2)

Useful Publications
Useful references include *Easy Access Australia* (available from PO Box 218, Kew VIC, 3101) and *Access for All* (National Parks & Wildlife Service, ☎ 9585 6444).

Language

Visitors from abroad who think Australian (that's 'Strine') is simply a weird variant of English/American will have a few surprises. For a start, many Australians don't even speak Australian – they speak Turkish, Greek, Chinese or Vietnamese.

English is the official and dominant language, but about 20% of people in Sydney use a different language at home.

Australian slang has become a standard part of the Australian language. Some classic Aussie expressions include:

arvo – afternoon
barbie – barbecue
beaut, beauty, bewdie – great
bloke – man
bludger – lazy person
bonza – great
BYO – Bring Your Own (booze to a restaurant, meat to a barbie)
crook – ill, substandard
dunny – outdoor lavatory
fair dinkum – honest
flat out – very busy or fast
g'day – traditional Australian greeting
mate – general term of familiarity, whether you know the person or not
mozzie – mosquito
ocker – an uncultivated or boorish Australian
ooroo – goodbye
piss – beer
sheila – woman
true blue – honest, genuine
tucker – food
yakka – work (from an Aboriginal language)

Richard I'Anson

Sydney – a bonza place for a barbie with a couple of mates.

Conversion Table

Clothing Sizes

Measurements approximate only; try before you buy.

Women's Clothing

Aust/NZ	8	10	12	14	16	18
Europe	36	38	40	42	44	46
Japan	5	7	9	11	13	15
UK	8	10	12	14	16	18
USA	6	8	10	12	14	16

Women's Shoes

Aust/NZ	5	6	7	8	9	10
Europe	35	36	37	38	39	40
France only	35	36	38	39	40	42
Japan	22	23	24	25	26	27
UK	3½	4½	5½	6½	7½	8½
USA	5	6	7	8	9	10

Men's Clothing

Aust/NZ	92	96	100	104	108	112
Europe	46	48	50	52	54	56
Japan	S		M	M		L
UK	35	36	37	38	39	40
USA	35	36	37	38	39	40

Men's Shirts (Collar Sizes)

Aust/NZ	38	39	40	41	42	43
Europe	38	39	40	41	42	43
Japan	38	39	40	41	42	43
UK	15	15½	16	16½	17	17½
USA	15	15½	16	16½	17	17½

Men's Shoes

Aust/NZ	7	8	9	10	11	12
Europe	41	42	43	44½	46	47
Japan	26	27	27.5	28	29	30
UK	7	8	9	10	11	12
USA	7½	8½	9½	10½	11½	12½

Weights & Measures

Length & Distance

1 inch = 2.54cm
1cm = 0.39 inches
1m = 3.3ft
1ft = 0.3m
1km = 0.62 miles
1 mile = 1.6km

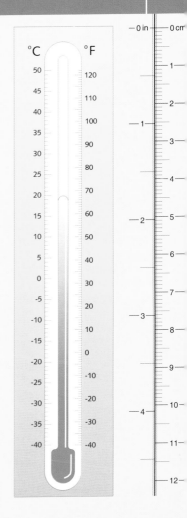

Weight

1kg = 2.2lb
1lb = 0.45kg
1g = 0.04oz
1oz = 28g

Volume

1 litre = 0.26 US gallons
1 US gallon = 3.8 litres
1 litre = 0.22 imperial gallons
1 imperial gallon = 4.55 litres

THE AUTHORS

Nikki Hall

A confirmed urbanite, Nikki came into the world – credit card in hand – ready to shop. A former Sydney resident and frequent visitor, she is always struck by the city's mix of relaxed hedonism and brash industriousness. For this book she revisited her favourite haunts and grilled her pals (a grab bag of funky filmmakers, swanky stylists and celeb chefs) for their list of must-see shops, bars, cafes and clubs.

Dani Valent

If you could drink Sydney with a straw, Dani Valent would have drained buckets of the stuff. Hard yards of research left her with Bondi sand down her bathers, Mardi Gras sequins on her platform soles, Olympic fever, a raging macchiato addiction, bushwalker's blisters and a fine array of 'culcha vulcha' frocks and market-mooched unnecessaries.

ABOUT LONELY PLANET GUIDEBOOKS

The story begins with a classic travel adventure: Tony and Maureen Wheeler's 1972 journey across Europe and Asia to Australia. Useful information about the overland trail did not exist at that time, so Tony and Maureen published the first Lonely Planet guidebook to meet a growing need.

From a kitchen table, then from a tiny office in Melbourne, Australia, Lonely Planet has become the largest independent travel publisher in the world, an international company with offices in Melbourne, Oakland (USA), London (UK) and Paris (France).

Today there are over 400 titles, including travel guides, walking guides, language kits & phrasebooks, travel atlases, diving guides, restaurant guides and travel literature.

At Lonely Planet we believe that travellers can make a positive contribution to the countries they visit – if they respect their host communities and spend their money wisely. Since 1986 a percentage of the income from books has been donated to aid projects and human rights campaigns.

ABOUT THE CONDENSED GUIDES

Other Lonely Planet Condensed guides include *Amsterdam* (due July 2000), *California, Crete, London, New York City* and *Paris*.

ABOUT THIS BOOK

Series developed by Diana Saad • Edited by Emma Miller • Design by Andrew Weatherill • Layout by Trudi Canavan • Cover design by Guillaume Roux • Maps by Charles Rawlings-Way • Publishing Manager Mary Neighbour • Software engineering by Dan Levin • Olympics section written by Liz Filleul • Thanks to Janet Austin, Gabrielle Green, David Kemp, Jay Krantz, Clay Lucas, Penelope Richardson, Valerie Tellini, Tim Uden and Kerrie Williams.

LONELY PLANET ONLINE

www.lonelyplanet.com or AOL keyword: lp
Lonely Planet's award-winning Web site has insider info on hundreds of destinations from Amsterdam to Zimbabwe, complete with interactive maps and colour photographs. You'll also find the latest travel news, recent reports from travellers on the road, guidebook upgrades and a lively bulletin board where you can meet fellow travellers, swap recommendations and seek advice.

PLANET TALK

Our FREE quarterly printed newsletter is full of tips from travellers and anecdotes from Lonely Planet authors. Every issue is packed with up-to-date travel news and advice, and includes a postcard from Lonely Planet co-founder Tony Wheeler, mail from travellers, a look at life on the road through the eyes of a Lonely Planet author, topical health advice, prizes for the best travel yarn, news about forthcoming Lonely Planet events and a complete list of Lonely Planet books and products.

To join our mailing list, email us at: go@lonelyplanet.co.uk (UK, Europe and Africa residents); info@lonelyplanet.com (North and South America residents); talk2us@lonelyplanet.com.au (the rest of the world); or contact any Lonely Planet office.

COMET

Our FREE monthly email newsletter brings you all the latest travel news, features, interviews, competitions, destination ideas, travellers' tips & tales, Q&As, raging debates and related links. Find out what's new on the Lonely Planet Web site and which books are about to hit the shelves.

Subscribe from your desktop: www.lonelyplanet.com/comet

LONELY PLANET OFFICES

Australia
PO Box 617, Hawthorn, Victoria 3122
☎ 03 9819 1877 fax 03 9819 6459
email: talk2us@lonelyplanet.com.au

USA
150 Linden St, Oakland, CA 94607
☎ 510 893 8555 TOLL FREE: 800 275 8555
fax 510 893 8572
email: info@lonelyplanet.com

UK
10a Spring Place, London NW5 3BH
☎ 020 7428 4800 fax 020 7428 4828
email: go@lonelyplanet.co.uk

France
1 rue du Dahomey, 75011 Paris
☎ 01 55 25 33 00 fax 01 55 25 33 01
email: bip@lonelyplanet.fr
minitel: 3615 lonelyplanet

**World Wide Web: www.lonelyplanet.com or AOL keyword: lp
Lonely Planet Images: lpi@lonelyplanet.com.au**

index

See separate indexes for Places to Eat (p. 126), Places to Stay (p. 127), Shopping (p. 127) and Sights (p.128, includes map references)

PLACES TO EAT

PLACES TO STAY

SHOPPING

sights index